TALL TALES AND HALF TRUTHS
OF
CLAY ALLISON

★ ★

T0274804

DONNA BLAKE BIRCHELL

FOREWORD BY
JOHN LEMAY

THE
History
PRESS

Published by The History Press
Charleston, SC
www.historypress.com

Unless otherwise noted, all images are in the public domain.

First published 2023

Manufactured in the United States

ISBN 9781467151030

Library of Congress Control Number: 2022951575

For the Phenom of the Tomes, John LeMay,
whose amazing gifts as a writer are an inspiration to us all.
You are a Blessing in my life.

CONTENTS

FOREWORD

Clay Allison is an enigma among gunfighters. Though he had far more adventures and battles than Billy the Kid and a longer, more storied life than Jesse James, Allison just doesn't have the same clout. There are no Clay Allison museums; he never fought Dracula or Frankenstein's daughter on the silver screen and, for that matter, never had a single film devoted to him. Perhaps Allison's lack of fame is a result of his less than glorious death—being thrown from a buckboard—rather than being assassinated or "going out in a blaze of glory" as did his peers.

The mundane way Clay Allison died was a shame for his legend. Others thought so, too, and took it upon themselves to color his death with a supernatural air. One fictitious rendition blamed the famous ghost steer, Old Ruidoso, for spooking Allison's mule team and pulling his wagon. That was the reason, they said, that he careened to his death into an arroyo, snapping his neck. In real life, it was probably a simple accident (or maybe Clay was just drunk again). In any case, it was that account of his death that intrigued me where a potential book for Allison was concerned. It also made me wonder, what other fabulous falsehoods are out there about Allison?

A few years back, I had tremendous fun in rounding up the more far-out folklore concerning Billy the Kid, such as his search for the Lost Adams Diggings, his alleged penchant for cross-dressing to hide from the law and his escape from the grave in general—all things that likely never happened, mind you. This collection of folklore resulted in *Tall Tales and Half Truths of Billy the Kid* (The History Press). I had so much fun that I immediately set out to do the same with Billy's gravedigger, Pat Garrett. Thus came *Tall Tales and Half Truths of Pat Garrett*. In my feverish quest for more far-out folklore to continue the series, I eventually came across Clay Allison. His life was insane. He was far more interesting in some regards than any gunfighter who ever lived, despite being less famous. As such, I decided he was perfect for the next book in the "Tall Tales and Half Truths" series.

But life got in the way, and the Clay Allison tome never quite came together. (In fact, as far as I got was two paragraphs that I reused in this foreword!) And that's when I thought of my friend Donna Blake Birchell. Donna and I both emerged as published writers and historians around the same time and became fast friends. What she did in Eddy County, I did in Chaves County, and vice versa. Book signings together eventually led to coauthoring *Hidden History of Southeast New Mexico* as well as talk of other projects we have yet to finish. At some point, I mentioned to her the Clay Allison project I abandoned and told her she should take it up if she wanted. To my joy, she did. You see, I'm one of those who writes books because I want to read them. I wanted to read *Tall Tales and Half Truths of Clay Allison*. Now I'm thrilled I can do just that. So, thank you, Donna, for picking up the trail of Clay Allison. I would have had fun digging up the dirt on Allison— and there is plenty of it. But I enjoyed reading Donna's book much more, and I know you will as well.

—Happy trails,
John LeMay

ACKNOWLEDGEMENTS

I t is with a full heart that I can say thank you once again to my dear friend Samantha Villa, who was instrumental in getting this journey rolling. I am so proud of your accomplishments, my friend!

My wonderful family continues to be my inspiration and rock. If it weren't for the encouragement of Jerry, Michael and Justin, this book would not exist. I know being a captive audience to my endless accounts of history is exhausting, but I am truly grateful for, and blessed by, your support! You are my strength. Saying thank you is not enough! All my love to you!

My grateful heart sends a huge thank-you to my friend and coauthor, John LeMay, for whom this book is dedicated, for being so gracious to gift this project to me so that his Tall Tales and Half Truth series could continue, and for writing the foreword. This type of selflessness and generosity in writers is extremely rare and greatly appreciated! You have helped in so many ways throughout this incredible journey, and I am so grateful for your friendship!

Amy McVay-Tellez is a name to know and remember! As historical director for the Historical Society of Southeastern New Mexico, Amy is a tireless one-woman dynamo who does so much to promote her stunning museum and the works of local authors. Amy is an absolute treasure whom I cannot say enough good things about. I am so proud to say that she is my dear friend! Blessings to you, Amy!

The staff members of the Haley Library in Midland, Texas, are priceless! Cathy Smith went above and beyond to peruse its archives to find information on Clay Allison for this book. It turns out that all the sources Cathy found were ones I had not seen, so I was ecstatic to receive this gold mine! It sent me down far more rabbit holes than I could imagine!

1
EARLY YEARS

Robert Andrew Clay Allison was a paradox of descriptions. He was mentally unstable yet a gentleman gunfighter, a hard drinker but a quiet-spoken man, a hell-raiser but an impromptu preacher. He could be mean as a rattlesnake but fiercely defended the innocent. Being one of the most dangerous gunmen in the West, Allison was deeply feared by those who knew of his prowess with a pistol or a Bowie knife, especially when he was "in his cups." For some reason, he has never received the attention even his lesser-known counterparts enjoyed. One can wonder about the results of an encounter, or even friendship, between Clay Allison and William Bonney or his Confederate counterpart Jesse James.

Please note the many outrageous and sometimes comical tall tales and half truths of Clay Allison's time on earth will be covered in this book, just not in chronological order. His nuances make him hard to pigeonhole into one smooth timeline.

One thing you could never call Clay Allison was an outlaw, although he did many things that skirted the gray line between legal and illegal. Clay, most likely named for his great-grandfather Robert Scotland Allison, had a Christian upbringing that made it extremely difficult for him to steal—difficult, but not impossible. He would borrow on several occasions but stated he was never a train robber or a horse thief and would staunchly defend himself with the help of his pistol if accused. Not too many people who disagreed with Clay Allison would live.

Over the years, many books and articles have been written about Clay Allison, as he preferred to be called, to varying degrees of accuracy, which is what we are going to explore in this book. As with any public figure, there are truths mixed in with rumors, some quite tragic or humorous, depending on the source. With Clay, it seems to depend on the source as to which description you will receive. Newspapers of the time had a field day with the gunfighter's antics, even leading to an attack by Allison on a newspaper office in response to an article which put him in a particularly bad light. But more on that later in this volume.

Allison was born on September 2, 1841, but even this date has come into question. Many have reported his birth to be in 1840, but family records point to 1841 as the correct year. One piece of information that has been repeated in nearly every book or article about Clay Allison is to the effect of, "Clay Allison's father died when Clay was only five years old." Through verification provided by census and death records, in fact, Jeremiah Scotland Allison (a Presbyterian minister) outlived his son by five years.

The Allison family tree, generally agreed on by family, reads like this: Father: Jeremiah Scotland (1811–1892); mother: Mariah Ruth (Brown) (1814–1894); siblings: Susan Elizabeth (1834–1866), Jesse Alonzo (1839–1904), Robert Clay (1841–1887), Jeremiah Monroe (1844–1887), Saluda Mary Ann (1846–1931), Emily Isabelle (1850–1933), Sarah Frances (1852–1934) and John William Allison (1854–1898).

One of the possible reasons for the confusion is the existence of multiple family trees online which state Robert Clay Allison's parents to be John (who coincidently was also a Presbyterian minister) and Nancy (Lemmond) Allison of Sugar Creek, North Carolina, but the Robert C. listed as their son was Robert Cyrus, not Clay. The Texas State Historical Association's *Handbook of Texas* confirms that Clay Allison's father was indeed Jeremiah Scotland Allison, so this is the source that will be held as true for this book.

Not much is written about what Clay's parents thought of his exploits or if they even knew of his activities in the West. Clay was said to have loved his mother, Mariah, dearly. She is claimed to have been a Cherokee in many histories of the Allison family. If Clay had not ventured into the cattle industry, he would have most likely become a minister like his father. Clay's youngest brother, John, and at times his brother Monroe, as he preferred to be called, did, however, follow him to the West to become ranching partners alongside their infamous brother, and together they amassed a sizeable number of cattle while stirring up a good amount of trouble along the way. Clay and John were known as two of the most respected cattlemen in Texas,

Colorado and New Mexico. Clay was most certainly John's mentor, while John was Clay's conscience. This combination made them a good team. Monroe would stick to the operations of the outfit.

Waynesboro, Tennessee, was home to the Allison family, which had a sheep and cattle ranch. Jeremiah "Jerry" S. Allison was on the minister circuit for Waynesboro and surrounding towns. The preacher and his wife were upstanding members of the community and raised their family with strong southern ideals and values that, in the world before the Civil War, were already ones of division. Tennessee had to struggle for statehood in a conflict with a much larger state at that time, North Carolina. After the Revolutionary War, North Carolina decided it did not want to deal with settlements in the far western reaches, so Tennessee was left to its own devices.

Wayne County was formed in 1817 and named after General "Mad" Anthony Wayne, who fought in the Revolutionary War. This county was settled by people from middle Tennessee and North and South Carolina who wanted to take advantage of the military grants, occupants' claims and warrants. The town of Waynesboro was formed in 1821 and would slowly grow to a population of 2,228 by the year 2000. It was there that a Confederate force of 1,800 men, including Robert Andrew Clay Allison, would cross the Tennessee River under the command of General Nathan Bedford Forrest on December 15, 1862.

Small farms dotted the Tennessee countryside, where cattle and sheep were raised to sustain families and the entire region. The Allison farm is where young Clay labored until his twenty-first year to help his father and where he sustained an injury that would forever change the course of his life.

As a young man, one story states, Clay was struck in the head by a mule's hoof. It is lucky for Clay he was resilient, as the grievous injury produced only migraines and momentary changes in personality. These changes would come into play to a great extent as Clay aged. The mule's kick could have easily ended Clay's life but instead left him with a deep crease in his skull, which most likely pressed on his brain, causing what we know today as traumatic brain injury. This injury can cause the victim to experience sudden spurts of violence, poor judgment and anger without warning. These symptoms have been repeatedly cited to describe Clay Allison's behavior throughout his adult years.

Other accounts of his injury have a sixteen-year-old Clay being thrown from a horse he was breaking and his head striking a rock, cracking the skull. He reportedly had a long recovery but was never the same. The young man became quiet, somber and at times violent—and crazy at other times. The seizures he was said to suffer later led Allison to become a dangerous and fierce soldier.

As the third of eight surviving children, Clay often took it upon himself to be the protector of the family, giving sage advice to his younger siblings, who looked up to their brother—and not just because he was over six feet tall. He was the strategist, the planner, the problem solver, one who was always scheming and was expert in getting out of messes he conjured up. Deep down, Clay knew he was not meant to settle in Tennessee. He wanted more.

2

REBEL IN SENTIMENT

You have been good soldiers; you can be good citizens.
Obey the laws, preserve your honor, and the government to which you have
surrendered can afford to be and will be magnanimous.
—Nathan B. Forrest, after his surrender in 1865

When the strife of a young America tore the nation apart during the Civil War, two members of the Allison family were in the thick of the troubles. At twenty years of age, Clay enlisted for one year in the Confederate army in the Tennessee Light Artillery division on October 15, 1861, under the command of Captain J.W. Eldridge. As a farmer's son, he was used to hard work and discipline, but he seemed to enjoy the actual art of warfare. It was reported his hatred for the Yankees was so great that when Clay's commander called a cease-fire after Union troops had retreated, Clay threatened to kill the commander and pursued the Northerners himself. This behavior would eventually earn the zealous young Confederate soldier a medical discharge. The camp doctor stated Clay was "incapable of performing the duties of a soldier because of a blow received many years ago, producing no doubt a depression of the skull. Emotional or physical excitement produces paroxysmal of a mixed character, partly epileptic and partly maniacal. He is suffering from such a paroxysmal caused by an attack of [illegible] during which he manifests an exact [illegible] to commit suicide."

Chances are, his commanding officers were delighted to be rid of the volatile young man, even though the Confederacy needed every available man. A family member, Clay Allison, wrote in his book *The Life and Death of a Gunfighter* about the life of his famous cousin in which he stated many of the outbursts, fights and threats Clay participated in while in the military were initiated by a bully who loved to antagonize the young Tennessee farmer. The constant taunts resulted in Clay acting out and reaping the punishments.

Other stories have appeared over the years. Some claim Clay never enlisted in the Confederate army at all but had a career as a bushwhacker and was hunted by the Union and the Confederacy alike. Once, it is said, Clay was pursued by the Confederates to his Tennessee home to be arrested for horse theft. The story has Allison and "his gang" holing up at the Allison farm, surrounded by soldiers. At the end of the day, none of the soldiers survived the melee, making Clay Allison and his gang wanted in Tennessee. Early newspaper articles describe Clay Allison as "a half-breed Indian—a leader of bushwhackers in Tennessee plundering rebel and union men impartially—guilty of all crimes in the calendars."

According to military records, Clay was included in the rosters of several other units during his first year, such as General William H. Jackson's artillery battery, Captain Palmer's Company, Light Artillery (Reneau Battery); Captain Phillips's Tennessee Light Artillery (Johnson Light Artillery) Company; Captain Polk's Battery, Light Artillery; and Captain Ramsey's Battery Artillery. It appears the Confederate army was having a difficult time finding a good fit for the volatile Tennessean.

Clay's younger brother Jeremiah Monroe, just eighteen years of age, served in many of the same units during this year. It was later reported Monroe was listed as a deserter, but those accusations have not been substantiated, as many Confederate soldiers were dispersed throughout the region. Just before the war ended, many returned home rather than surrender. John, the youngest of the Allison clan, only thirteen at the time, could not enlist, but that did not stop him from sneaking out of the house to collect his brothers after the end of the war, according to family lore.

Sympathies for the Confederacy were strong in Tennessee and in Clay's heart. He formed a deep hatred for the Union and for Northerners and their ideals. One of Clay's biggest character flaws, racism, led him into numerous situations where his extreme loathing of the Black race resulted in murders later deemed "self-defense." Clay Allison's beliefs and actions are extremely difficult to support with a modern-day mindset. It was a much different time, and atrocities were committed on both sides of the Mason-Dixon line.

General Nathan Bedford Forrest

Clay's first military experience may have been over with his discharge on January 15, 1861, but the young man reenlisted nine months later, on September 22, 1862, as a member of the Nineteenth Tennessee Cavalry, Company F, under Colonel Robert McCulloch, and then, just after his twenty-first birthday, with the more aggressive General Nathan Bedford Forrest, who was known as the "Wizard of the Saddle" in the Ninth Tennessee Cavalry, Company C. It was with this regiment that Clay found his calling and remained for the duration of the Civil War. Forrest's ruthless style of command suited Allison; both men were of like minds against the Union, Northerners and Blacks. As a result of this hatred, it is reported that Forrest, who made his living as a slave trader, was also the first Grand Wizard of the Ku Klux Klan. Clay later became a member of this racist organization for a short time, stirring up trouble as the Grand Cyclops in Tennessee, according to author Louis Serna in his book *Clay Allison and the Colfax County War*.

General Nathan Bedford Forrest was known as the "Wizard of the Saddle" for his riding skills.

Clay's admiration for Nathan Forrest was so great that he would continue to wear the Van Dyke–style mustache and beard that his mentor sported for the rest of his life. Forrest is said to have killed thirty men himself and was compared by a fellow Confederate to a "panther springing upon its prey and many Yankees feared him as the devil incarnate." This reputation caused fear in not only the Union forces but also in his own ranks. General William Tecumseh Sherman remarked on Forrest's "genius for strategy," which made the Confederate, in his eyes, one of the "most remarkable men of the Civil War."

Forrest was the only soldier from either faction to enlist as a private and rise to the rank of lieutenant general by the end of the war. Being a millionaire before the start of the war, Forrest funded many of the necessities needed for his troops himself. This tenacious general would also be the last Confederate commander east of the Mississippi River to surrender, one month after the meeting of General in Chief of the Armies of the Confederate States, Robert E. Lee, and Union general Ulysses S. Grant at Appomattox in April 1865.

Allison was said to have participated in thirteen of the most legendary and bloody battles of the Civil War under Forrest's command. Some of these conflicts included the Battle of Chickamauga, the Battle of Brice's Crossroads, the Battle of Tupelo, the Battle of Franklin, the Third Battle of Murfreesboro, the Battle of Nashville and the Battle of Selma. One atrocious incident would follow Bedford Forrest for the rest of his life: the Battle of Fort Pillow.

FORT PILLOW MASSACRE

The Fort Pillow Massacre took place on April 12, 1864, in Tennessee. General Nathan B. Forrest's troops, numbering close to 2,500, surrounded the fort to negotiate a surrender. But when Union major Lionel Booth was killed by a Confederate sniper's bullet, the chaos began. The second in charge, Major William Bradford, a native-born Tennessean, asked for a one-hour cease-fire in the hopes that reinforcements would arrive down the river.

When the Union boats were sighted, Forrest's men stormed the fort and easily overran the military establishment, resulting in over three hundred Union soldiers taken as prisoners of war. As most of the captured soldiers were Black and fighting for the Union, this sealed their awful fate. Forrest ordered the prisoners to be killed rather than exchanged. Under a flag of truce, Forrest wrote a message to the Union forces, "Your gallant defense of Fort Pillow has entitled you to the treatment of brave men," and he continued to demand unconditional surrender with assurances of the garrison. Forrest did not wait until the message was returned before he advanced on the fort.

Union forces were taken by surprise and forced back into the river while engaging in hand-to-hand combat. The resistance collapsed under the continual charge of the Confederate soldiers. Captured Union soldiers were clubbed, bayonetted or gunned down without mercy after they had laid down their arms. Forrest's troops sustained fourteen casualties and eighty-six wounded men for his efforts. The Federal troops lost half of their strength, with 64 percent of the Black troops lost and 30 percent of the White troops. The Union soldiers were not the only victims of this melee, as the Tennessee Confederates turned on their own whom they considered turncoats to the cause.

The brutal slaughter of unarmed Union soldiers created a huge controversy then that continues today, in addition to being judged a very

Fort Pillow was the site of one of the most horrific battles in the American Civil War.

bloody episode in the Civil War. Union accounts tell of a horrible war crime, a determination later supported by a lengthy federal investigation. Confederate accounts differed; Forrest claimed his troops did nothing wrong, as Major Bradford refused to surrender.

One report stated Major Bradford was seen fleeing toward Mississippi as his garrison was destroyed; another said he was one of the causalities. His reported date of death, April 14, 1864, supports the account that Bradford was shot and killed while trying to escape from the Confederate soldiers near Brownsville, Tennessee, and was buried in an unmarked grave. This occurrence earned Nathan Forrest vilification from the press, who called him "Butcher Forrest." He denied the charges until his death, but the horrific actions still haunt his name today. Fort Pillow is now known as Fort Pillow State Historic Park.

CONFEDERATE SPY

Serving as a scout and spy under General Forrest, Clay was reported to have been captured, tried and sentenced to death on his first mission, but this may not be correct. Clay was clever and knew the countryside in his home state and surrounding states very well. According to a story by John Simkin, Clay was "captured at Shiloh but managed to escape," but according to records, Allison, although part of Forrest's company that finally surrendered on May 4, 1865, was not treated as a prisoner of war but as a spy and was sentenced to be executed by firing squad in Gainesville, Alabama.

Clay Allison was a tall man, said to be anywhere between five foot nine and six foot two inches in height, depending on the sources. But he was said to have small hands, often compared to those of a woman by many biographers, and this allowed him to escape the bonds of his shackles (much as the outlaw Billy the Kid was said to have done in Lincoln, New Mexico). This escape allowed Clay to kill his guard and flee the night before his scheduled execution on May 11, 1865. There is a disagreement among historians if this event of his escape took place; some accounts have Clay slipping away to join guerrilla forces when Forrest surrendered. Not much is written about these years.

Accounts by Jeremiah Monroe Allison have Clay imprisoned on Johnson's Island in Sandusky Bay off Lake Erie, from which he made his escape by swimming ashore on the eve of his execution. But there is no record of this with the U.S. War Department. According to its records, Clay was a prisoner in Alabama from May 4 through May 10, 1865. Unfortunately, many of these records have been lost over the years. In any case, Clay was able to survive the Civil War and go on to create havoc in the Southwest.

Confederate troops led by General Forrest were paroled by Union general Edward Canby, who also played a significant role in the Battle of Valverde

and the Battle of Glorieta Pass (known as the Gettysburg of the West) as the commander of the Department of New Mexico—which ironically would become Clay's future home. Forrest's men were the last Confederate troops east of the Mississippi to surrender. The house where the parole took place, known as the Ellis house, was later established as a monument to General Forrest.

The dangerous 240-mile journey back to Tennessee from Alabama took weeks, whereas today this trek can be made in about four hours. It was during this trip that Clay had plenty of time to contemplate his future. He

It was well known that most Confederate soldiers were proficient with both firearms and knives.

knew he was not cut out to be a farmer. He wanted to be a cattle rancher. Besides, there were too many northerners in the region for his liking.

The rights of Confederate soldiers were limited after the war, with pardons not given until 1868. The only means of transportation home was to walk. Catching a train or steamship or obtaining a horse were extremely rare opportunities. Many returning Confederates died from starvation. To fight hunger, looting was commonplace. The Civil War would come to be known and referred to as the "Lost Cause" in the South.

The Union army handed out haversacks containing a small amount of hardtack (an unleavened biscuit made from flour, water and salt), a ration still used today. Ideally, one dunks the cracker into water or coffee and then crumbles up the pieces into a skillet of fried bacon to soften. These hard morsels obtained many nicknames over the years: "tooth duller," "worm castles," "armor plates" and "dog biscuits." They are not particularly appetizing names, but if you were starving, these pieces of food were considered a three-course meal.

On his journey home, Clay was said to have been assisted by a Union soldier, Pete Montana of New York, who was assigned by the army to follow Allison home. Trust between the two men was sketchy in the beginning, but after a few meals and conversations, the two were able to establish a mutual trust. Clay found that the soldier abandoned him toward the end of their journey but was kind enough to leave Allison a horse with full saddlebags, a change of clothes, a Henry repeating rifle, a new army revolver six-shooter in a holster and a Grimsley saddle. All of this was far more valuable than the fourteen dollars in compensation given to Allison by the United States Army.

3

GOOD-NATURED HOLY TERROR

Clay Allison was not a gunfighter, but a stockman with the ability to kill.
—F. Stanley

He'd made the reputation that comes when fellers shoot.
—J. Frank Dobie

Post–Civil War America was greatly changed from the status quo of a mere five years earlier. Brother had fought against brother; families were torn apart by different beliefs or by great losses suffered as multiple family members were either dead or maimed. The viciousness of the war was unsurpassed. Guerrilla warfare had been utilized to its fullest extent, mainly by extreme factions of the Confederate army.

Brutality connected to names such as William C. Quantrill, William "Bloody Bill" Anderson, James "Grim Chieftain" Lane, John "The Gray Ghost" Mosby, Charles Jennison and John McNeill are prime examples of the cruelty perpetrated by both sides during this gruesome chapter in American history. From this period emerged some of the most famous figures in the Old West: Jesse and Frank James, Cole Younger and Robert Clay Allison.

Allison was rumored to be the leader of his own guerrilla faction after the Civil War. Its members were known to be ruthless terrorists, according to newspaper articles of the time. Having followed his mentor, Nathan

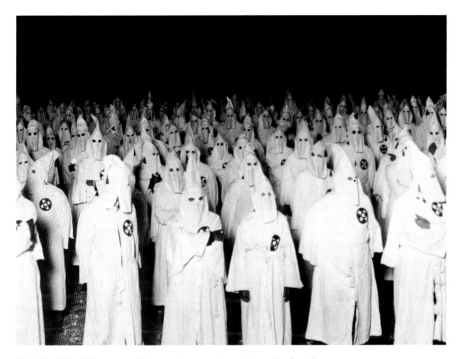

The Ku Klux Klan spread hate and terror throughout the South.

Forrest, into the secret society of the Ku Klux Klan, Clay saw nothing wrong with his actions, viewing them as an extension of the war which had not been completed in his mind. Those actions included serving as the aforementioned Grand Cyclops and conducting raids in the Tennessee countryside. Clay's ideals would also play a large part in some of his most brutal actions in the future.

Clay Allison was said to have been thought of as a Robin Hood–type character during wartime. One illustration of this involved a group of guerrillas led by Allison and some Federal soldiers who battled at the home of a widow. During this melee, two of the woman's mules were killed. When Clay heard of this, he made his way into the Federal officer's tent and forced the man to promise, albeit at gunpoint, to pay the widow the full value of the animals. There is nothing written to indicate the man kept his promise, but if he continued to live after this incident, we can only surmise that he did. Clay's killer reputation was well known even then.

CLAY'S FIRST CIVILIAN KILL

After escaping from Gainesville, Alabama, in 1865, Clay faced many hazards on the way home. Eluding Union officers was his main concern. Although the war was officially over, the conflict was not over in the minds of soldiers on both sides, especially as Confederates were not considered veterans. Once Clay was finally able to make it home with the aid of Pete Montana, he attempted to settle into a "normal" life on the family farm. Success was probably impossible, given the climate of the times, and Clay had already experienced several violent incidents on his way home.

While working in a nearby family field, Clay heard his mother scream. Immediately coming to her rescue, he found a Union corporal from the Third Illinois Cavalry harassing her by demanding to seize the farm. As an intimidation method, the laughing corporal picked up a prized glass or ceramic pitcher and smashed it on the porch. Incensed, Clay instinctively acted, using his ever-present rifle, leaving the rude soldier crumpled in a pool of his own blood on the Allison porch. Realizing more Union soldiers were around who may have heard the rifle shot, the Allison family acted quickly to remove any evidence of the soldier's visit. They finished in the nick of time, as a group of Union soldiers did indeed show up just as the family had feared to investigate the gunfire. Convinced that the family had no idea where their fellow soldier was, the northerners moved on, even if suspicious.

Other historians wrote that Jeremiah Allison, Clay's father, had been long since deceased and was not able to help with the fracas. In truth, the elder Allison was also clearing a field but had not heard the scuffle. It was evident Tennessee was becoming too dangerous for Clay Allison to stay. He was encouraged by his parents to go to Texas for a new life. He knew if he lingered on the farm, he would bring more peril to his family. The decision was made to move to Texas with his brothers Monroe and John, sister Mary and brother-in-law Lewis G. Coleman. Cattle ranching was of greater interest to Clay than farming anyway. Besides, there were fewer northerners to contend with in Texas. Clay was and would remain the epitome of the southern plantation gentleman in thoughts and actions, raising fear in those he opposed.

TEXAS BOUND

The journey from Waynesboro, Tennessee, to the Brazos River in Texas, more than 750 miles (by today's estimations), took months to complete, especially with several hundred head of cattle in tow. The experience Clay gained from this trip would serve him well in his later endeavors, as he was able to live in Kansas, Missouri and Texas along the way. These states later served as locations for his homes, as well as locations for some of Clay's most outrageous antics.

Employed by his brother-in-law Lewis Coleman, Clay was sent to the New Mexico Territory as a collections agent to recover monies owed to the ranch owner. Tom Stockton of the V7 Ranch and a man known only as Mr. Wilborn were the first names on his list. When approached by Allison, Stockton promised to get the money owed within a couple of weeks, but he managed to abscond, leaving Wilborn alone to face Clay's wrath. Scores were settled, and Tom Stockton, who later owned the Clifton House, became fast friends with Clay in the future.

Clay's early head injury was exacerbated later in life when he not only discovered alcohol but also found that he could consume copious quantities of the amber liquid without much consequence—at least to himself. This discovery led to many pranks and eventual deaths. When Clay's eyes drew dark and his face changed from melancholy to dangerously serious while he was enjoying his whiskey, cowboys knew to keep their distance, as his volatile reputation was legendary, and he could turn vicious at the drop of a hat.

Allison was probably one of the most observed gunfighters of his time, as people would intently watch his ever-changing tones for a hint of what the cowman was thinking. It became a good practice for other saloon patrons to walk on eggshells around the tall, moody rancher if they wanted to continue to breathe. Saloon owners would gauge how many lanterns and how much glassware they would lose because of Clay's ever-changing moods.

One legend is widely told of an encounter Clay had with a ferryman by the name of Zachary Colbert (others have written his name as Benjamin Franklin Colbert, a Chickasaw) at the Red River Crossing near Denison, Texas, which was known as the gateway to Texas. Colbert recognized an opportunity to make a few extra coins when he saw the large Allison party arrive at his ferry. Colbert's Ferry was an important crossing on the Red River, providing passage for the Butterfield Overland Mail as well as those traveling west between the years of 1853 and 1899. Confederate troops also utilized this service to move from Texas to the Indian Territory, now known as Oklahoma.

Ferries were the only way to cross rivers before bridges were installed.

The going rate in 1872 for a river crossing, according to the *Encyclopedia of Oklahoma History and Culture*, was "one dollar for a two-horse wagon, one dollar and twenty-five cents for a four-horse wagon, one dollar and fifty cents for a six-horse wagon, twenty-five cents for a man and horse and ten cents a head for cattle or horse." These prices were whether you rode on the ferry or not. The Allison party consisted of five people, some horses, cattle and a couple of wagons. They crossed into the state of Texas around 1863 on their way to the Brazos River.

Halfway across the river, legend has it, Colbert decided to up his fare significantly. This did not sit well with Clay. Colbert would not negotiate with Allison and knew he had the family in a predicament, as they were already on the water. Clay decided to teach the ferryman a hard lesson in fairness by, it is said, nearly beating the man to death. The only thing that saved Colbert from being killed is when both men fell into the Red River, which cooled the temper of Allison enough for the ferryman to escape.

In a July 22, 1887 article in the *Range* (written after Clay's death), it was reported that Clay killed Colbert in a sensational knife fight on the ferry. In Clay's flair for the dramatic, the two men battled using Bowie knives with their left hands bound behind their backs. Zachary Colbert then died from his wounds. But the consensus has it that Clay left Colbert severely beaten and unconscious, with a lesson learned not to mess with this man from Tennessee. Either way, this encounter came back to haunt Clay in a later episode in 1874.

GOODNIGHT-LOVING TRAIL BLAZER

One of Clay's first jobs in his new home was as a cattle drover with a Texas rancher from Tennessee, Marcus L. Dalton, in the Brazos River region. He also worked for his brother-in-law Lewis Coleman, driving cattle from Texas

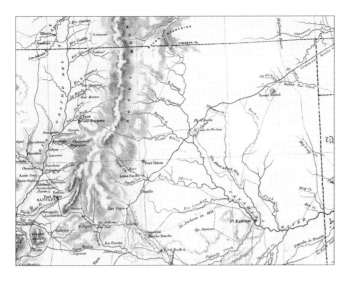

Charles Goodnight drove his cattle throughout the vast grasslands of northern New Mexico.

into the New Mexico Territory grasslands. It was with both outfits that Clay honed his skills with cattle and later landed him a more lucrative position with cattle baron Charles Goodnight as a drover along the Goodnight-Loving Trail.

In 1866, Allison signed on with Goodnight and his partner, Oliver Loving, as part of a huge movement of longhorn cattle and helped to blaze the now-famous Goodnight-Loving Trail from Young County, Texas, southwest to Horsehead Crossing near Red Bluff, on the Pecos River. The trail then continued to Fort Sumner in New Mexico and then north into Colorado. This trail would eventually be extended into Wyoming.

It is written that Clay was one of the eighteen original drovers on the Goodnight-Loving Trail bringing two thousand head of cattle into Fort Sumner, New Mexico, and to the Bosque Redondo, where between eight thousand and ten thousand Navajo and Mescalero Apache tribe members were housed in deplorable conditions during the Civil War. Demand for provisions was extremely high, as the government had not planned for this number of residents when the roundup of Native Americans began.

BOSQUE REDONDO

The Navajo, who were living in the northwestern New Mexico Territory, were burned out of their homes and crops by Christopher "Kit" Carson under the orders of General James Carleton as part of an experiment in the control of Native tribes. The four-hundred-mile forced walk was known as the "Long Walk" by the Navajo, who lost nearly twenty-five hundred members of their tribe as they covered on foot the entire span of the New Mexico Territory in the winter months of 1863–64. Several marches occurred between 1863 and 1866 in which a reported nine thousand Navajo people were captured or recaptured after escape and returned to the Bosque Redondo on the Pecos River.

Five hundred Mescalero Apache were also brought to Fort Sumner from their home in the White Mountains near present-day Ruidoso, New Mexico—a forced trek of nearly two hundred miles. They were being relocated to participate in a farming project, something the Mescalero Apache hated. Beef was greatly needed in this newly formed community of enemies, so Goodnight was able to sell most of his herd in Fort Sumner while Loving continued to Colorado.

The experiment failed miserably due to several factors. Mainly, the two tribes were enemies and had different lifestyles and rituals. Starvation and smallpox reduced significantly the populations during their six years of captivity. The Mescalero Apache, a warrior tribe, were not willing to assimilate to the farming way of life and executed an escape plan in November 1863 in which they lit their normal night fires in the camp and simply left. The government did not pursue the tribe to their homes at this time, since they were greatly overpopulated in Bosque Redondo as

Beginning as a social experiment, Bosque Redondo would be the final resting place for hundreds of people.

it was. It was not until June 1868 that the Navajos were allowed to return home in the Four Corners region of the territory. Although the events were massively tragic, both tribes have since flourished and are among the largest in the nation.

Bose Ikard

Interestingly, the trail boss on this journey was Mississippi-born Bose Ikard, a freed slave and Black man whom Charles Goodnight trusted without a doubt and the cattlemen held in high regard. Although racial tensions were high at this time, it is thought that Goodnight's esteem for the drover was the reason Ikard did not have any trouble from Allison. It is certain that Goodnight would have tolerated no hostilities toward his trusted friend. Goodnight once said of his trail boss, "Ikard surpassed any man I had in endurance and stamina. He was my detective, banker [since no one would suspect a Black man to be carrying large amounts of money] and everything in Colorado, New Mexico and the other wild country I was in. We went through some terrible trials during those four years on the trail."

When Bose Ikard passed away in Weatherford, Texas, in 1929 at the age of eighty-one on the Parker Ranch, Charles Goodnight ordered an upright marker for his friend's grave. It read: "Served with me four years on the Goodnight-Loving Trail, never shirked a duty or disobeyed an order, rode with me in many stampedes, participated in three engagements with Comanches, splendid behavior."

One of the engagements with Comanche involved the famed warrior Quanah Parker after Bose returned to Texas from Colorado, where he lived with his wife, Angeline, and "at least six children." Ikard was honored with a star on the Texas Trail of Fame at the Fort Worth Stockyards in 1997. A Texas state historical marker was erected at Bose Ikard's gravesite—a great tribute indeed.

Oliver Loving

In July 1867, near present-day Loving, New Mexico, the Goodnight-Loving group was attacked by a group of Comanche. Before this attack, Oliver Loving and a drover named "One Arm" Bill Wilson scouted north closer to where

The town of Loving, New Mexico, is named after Charles Goodnight's partner, Oliver Loving.

the town of Eddy (now known as Carlsbad) would be established and were ambushed by the Comanche at Wildcat Bluff. Wilson and Loving survived the gun battle, although Oliver Loving received what would play out to be a mortal gunshot wound.

Loving was taken north by Bill Wilson to the nearest medical facility, in Fort Sumner, approximately 160 miles from Eddy. Once in Fort Sumner, Loving was given the option of having his arm amputated, but he staunchly refused. This refusal would cost him his life, as gangrene quickly set in. Loving's death devastated Goodnight, who, it was said, carried a photo of Loving in his pocket for many years.

It was Loving's last request that Goodnight take his body from Fort Sumner to Weatherford, Texas, for burial. This arduous journey of over 450 miles is said to be the basis for the 1989 epic miniseries *Lonesome Dove*.

Clay soon achieved an excellent reputation as a cattle drover and was sought out by many ranchers to head their herds. While working as a trail boss for Marcus L. Dalton from 1867 to 1869 and then for his brother-in-law Lewis Coleman and his partner, Irwin W. Lacy, who had quickly established themselves as cattle legends in Texas, Clay was paid with three hundred head of cattle to establish his own herd after a cattle drive.

During the cattle drives with the Goodnight-Loving team and for Coleman, Clay was exposed to the beauty of the Cimarron Valley of northern New Mexico. Lush, green pasturelands flanked by tall palisades and mountains are nothing short of breathtaking. Elk, deer, bear, mountain lion and fish were all plentiful, and the grazing possibilities seemed endless. It was at this time that Clay decided he would eventually have a ranch in this promised land. A move to the New Mexico Territory would be the start of a raucous new adventure for the burgeoning cattleman.

Clay's Vermejo Ranch on the Poñil Creek, close to the New Mexico and Colorado border, was on some of the most desirable rangelands in the region and is now owned by movie mogul Ted Turner. Tall grass pastures did well in fattening up the cattle for sale, but according to Roswell historian Maurice Fulton, Clay's cattle did not take to the area, so he sold off the remainder and moved back to the Brazos River ranch to start over once again.

DEADLY DUEL

After Clay's time on the Goodnight-Loving Trail, he set up his own ranch along the Brazos River. Here, one of the most sensational events to start the legend of Clay Allison was reported to have occurred in 1870. In a waterhole dispute with a neighbor, Clay came to be linked to a highly debated event. Water is a priceless commodity in the Southwest, and rights are strictly enforced. The theft of two items in the Old West could get you killed: a horse and water.

Keep in mind that no official early records, such as newspaper accounts, exist of the following encounter, but it did appear in many later legends told of the gunfighter in his early days, so there may be some truth to the story.

While riding the range of his Texas ranch, Clay happened upon a herd of cattle utilizing one of his watering holes. These cattle were not a part of his herd. Recognizing the brand as his neighbor, known only to history as Johnson, Clay confronted the rancher, who stated that he saw no fencing to prevent his cattle from watering there. After a heated discussion, it was decided, for some inexplicable reason (Clay was said to have made the decision), that the "fair" way to settle the argument (in true Clay Allison fashion) was for both men to dig a grave, strip off their shirts and proceed with a knife fight to the death inside the grave. It was agreed ahead of the duel that the winner would have rights to the watering hole and was to give the loser a proper burial. Personally, it makes no sense Johnson would agree to this match, especially given the fact that Allison was known to be as skilled with his prized Bowie knife as he was with a firearm.

After an intense fight, Clay's leg was severely lacerated, a wound that would remain with the gunfighter for the rest of his life, causing a noticeable limp. But Clay fared better of the two men, as this ground in Texas was the site of a fresh grave—for Mr. Johnson. Wanting to do the proper thing given his background, Clay filled in the hole, said a few words over the grave and left to tend to his wound. The Johnson family was reported to have been furious with this action and accused Clay of murder, as there were no witnesses.

It is thought guilt from this fight and consideration of how valiantly Johnson fought would lead Clay to bouts of deep remorse. Other historians believe this never happened and, if it did, Allison would not have killed his neighbor, but the one left standing with the fewest wounds would be declared the winner, and the loser would move on.

Many believe Allison did indeed kill Johnson, and the family vowed revenge on the gunfighter for the death of their relative. The Johnson family may have had a hand in Clay's mysterious death many years later. Many say Allison sold his ranch on the Brazos River for less than it was worth and sent the money to Johnson's family before moving to New Mexico. It is ironic that three years after Clay's death, his widow, Dora, married a man named Jesse Lee Johnson. If Clay fled, he did not seem to be too worried, as he brought a large herd of cattle with him after the incident and the going was slow.

According to historian Maurice Fulton, Clay was partial to duels, especially using a Bowie knife. He is thought to have fought two more, although undocumented, with residents in the Indian Territory when he moved to the region. Clay was said to be very well known to the residents of the Indian Territory, giving credence to the belief of several historians that Clay's mother, Mariah, was Cherokee. This may be why Clay was accepted by the Native population—although he would not hesitate to gun down a Native warrior if he deemed it necessary.

4

THE COLFAX COUNTY WAR

Anyone who knows New Mexico history is probably aware of the Lincoln County War, which began in 1878 with the death of John H. Tunstall. For unknown reasons, the deadlier Colfax County War, which started in earnest with the 1875 death of Reverend Franklin J. Tolby, a Methodist circuit rider, was pushed to the wayside in the historical record.

The Lincoln County War even garnered the attention of President Benjamin Harrison, who declared the main street in Lincoln to be the "deadliest street in America." The primary conflict lasted for five months, beginning on February 18, 1878, until July 20, 1878, but it continued sporadically until 1881 with the death of Billy the Kid. Although tragic, fewer than twenty lives were taken during this war. On the other hand, the Colfax County War lasted fifteen years and cost the lives of over two hundred people.

While the two wars differed in terms of number of combatants and casualties, the primary reason behind both was greed. Land, wealth and status were all factors. In the case of the Colfax County War, 1,714,764.93 acres of land were at stake, so the greed was immense. The next sections of text illustrate the main causes that contributed to the conflict now known as the bloody Colfax County War.

MAXWELL LAND GRANT

The land included in the Maxwell Land Grant first belonged to the Jicarilla Apache tribe and was claimed in 1524 by the Spanish government. In 1821, the Mexican government, which controlled the territory, kept the Spanish policy of establishing land grants to encourage settlers' migration to the region. This land encompassed over one million acres in northern New Mexico and southern Colorado. In 1841, these acres were part of the largest contiguous private landholding in U.S. history. The New Mexico Territory was described as "wild as hell on a greased pole" during these early days.

A French Canadian trapper, Charles Beaubien, who became a Mexican citizen, and his partner, Guadalupe Miranda, the secretary to Governor Manuel Armijo, petitioned for a land grant in 1841. The grant was approved, but on the condition that the men swear to colonize and cultivate their land. After two years, the men had not lived up to their end of the bargain, but they were able to get a justice of the peace in Taos to sign an order promising them full possession of the land.

Explorer and trapper Lucien Bonaparte Maxwell arrived in the area in 1849 and married Charles Beaubien's daughter Luz. Well respected by all, Lucien soon became a highly successful man. He and Luz owned a home in Rayado, New Mexico, and a large home in Cimarron, along the Mountain Branch of the Santa Fe Trail that brought in a good income for the couple. They also later owned a large, two-story home in Fort Sumner.

During this time, settlers were moving in on the land, basically becoming squatters. Clay Allison's Vermejo ranch, which was located at the junction of the Vermejo and Canadian Rivers, nine miles north of Springer, New Mexico, was part of this group of settlers. It has been written Clay would eventually purchase his ranch from Maxwell, making him one of the earliest settlers in the region. Allison's brand was the Circle Box. When gold was found on the land grant, Maxwell began charging the squatters twelve dollars a year to live on his land. He was not successful in collecting these fees in most cases. Clay also tried his hand at gold mining in Willow Creek near his ranch but decided that cattle ranching was a much more lucrative occupation.

Lucien was said to have a kind heart, illustrated in the story of Delvina Maxwell. Of Apache descent, Delvina was captured by the Ute tribe, which enslaved her. As the Ute traveled through Maxwell's land in the Cimarron Valley, Maxwell was a witness to the brutal treatment of the girl. He offered to pay the captors for her and struck a bargain with the tribe for two bulls

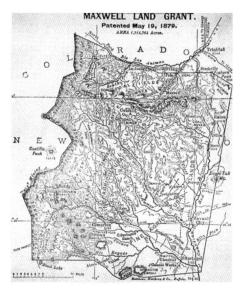

Left: The Maxwell Land Grant reportedly encompassed nearly two million acres of prime land.

Right: Lucien B. Maxwell was a true rags-to-riches success story.

and a goat in exchange for the Apache girl. Delvina was adopted by the Maxwell family and provided care for his children and grandchildren for the rest of her life.

Maxwell later had his land grant taken from him through corrupt dealing of his attorney, Frank Springer, to the benefit of the U.S. government for railroad land and to his own benefit. Land for the town of Springer was also obtained through this deal. The Maxwells sold the land in 1870 to Senator Jerome Chaffie for $650,000. Chaffie then immediately sold the land to a group of English financiers for $1.35 million. They in turn sold out to a Dutch company six months later.

Lucien Maxwell sold all of his other assets for an additional $100,000 and moved first to Santa Fe and then to Fort Sumner, where he bought the old Fort Sumner buildings and land for $5,000 in 1871 to live out the rest of his days. It is at this house, then owned by Lucien's son Pete Maxwell, that Sheriff Pat Garrett shot the outlaw William H. Bonney (Billy the Kid) on July 14, 1881. Bonney is buried within thirty feet of the great landowner and his family in the Fort Sumner cemetery.

The Dutch company, aware of the history of the resources on the land grant, immediately opened a land office, expecting to be overrun with

Right: Fort Sumner, New Mexico, boasts being the final resting place of outlaw Billy the Kid. *Courtesy author's collection.*

Below: Lucien Bonaparte Maxwell had several houses in the territory, including at Fort Sumner and Cimarron.

purchasers. They never showed, due to the contributing factors of the dropping price of gold, the Santa Fe Trail then being underutilized before the advancements of the railroad and the constant threat of attacks from local Indigenous peoples.

The Maxwell Land Grant and Railway Company was then formed, and a push to rid the land of squatters began in earnest. Those occupying the land felt they had unwritten permission from Maxwell to remain on the land grant, especially as they had been living there for thirty years. The struggle to remove the squatters became the focus of the Santa Fe Ring, which had its own designs on how the land should be used.

Force, in the form of hired gunslingers and local law enforcement, was utilized, and this caused a few squatters to stand up against the corrupt Santa Fe Ring, which also leveled false accusations against the settlers. One of the strongest opponents was Methodist preacher Franklin J. Tolby, who gave blazing sermons in the churches along the Cimarron Valley against the evils of the Santa Fe Ring and was seen openly arguing with Ring member Joseph Palen, who warned the parson to cease or move out of the country.

Retaliations for the sheriff-delivered eviction notices began with the Maxwell Grant pastures being set aflame and continuing with an increase in cattle rustling and officials being threatened at gunpoint. These actions were met with nighttime raids on the ranches to "encourage cooperation" with the grant landowners. As a result, the killing commenced, and the Colfax County War was born.

SANTA FE RING

Corrupt politics has always played a role in the history of New Mexico. One of the most powerful groups practicing corruption was known as the Santa Fe Ring. Businessmen, landowners and politicians all the way up to the governor were highly influential in the control of the New Mexico Territory. To defy them was to sign a death warrant. The Santa Fe Ring was thought have started both the Colfax County War and the Lincoln County War with the assassinations of Reverend Franklin J. Tolby and John H. Tunstall, respectively.

In *New Mexico's Troubled Years: The Story of the Early Territorial Governors*, Calvin Horn writes: "The worst of the violence came after the September 1875 murder of the Reverend F.J. Tolby, whom many Colfax County residents believed was killed for interfering with attempts by the Santa Fe Ring to control the Maxwell Land Grant Co. and the county." Before the murder of Tolby, Allison had been an at-large tool of the Ring, but with Tolby's death laid at the feet of the men from New Mexico's territorial capital, Allison switched sides and took a fierce part in the rebellion of the settler-citizens of Colfax County against the powerful Santa Fe Ring.

Knowing Clay Allison's dangerous reputation, the Santa Fe Ring had eagerly courted the gunfighter to join their circle, even though he was one of the squatters they despised. Allison went along with the Ring for a short while, carefully riding the fence, until the death of Reverend Tolby. Allison's father was a Presbyterian circuit rider in Tennessee, and Clay had great respect for the preacher. His death was unforgiveable in Clay's eyes.

When the young parson did not return home to his family in Elizabethtown from his scheduled travels, he was discovered murdered in Cimarron Canyon on September 17, 1875. Since Tolby had made himself an enemy of the Santa Fe Ring–owned Maxwell Land Grant Company with his frequent, highly damning letters to New York newspapers, in which he divulged names and activities of the unethical group, blame immediately went in that direction. Tolby was known to have opposed the appointment of Samuel Axtell for governor of the New Mexico Territory—he had backed Methodist minister Joseph Brooks of Arkansas, which angered Axtell. According to historian Philip Rasch, "Tolby openly quarreled with Joseph Palen and was warned by him that he had better cease his criticisms of the Santa Fe Ring or leave the country." Palen was a powerful judge and a high-ranking member of the Ring.

The murder of Reverend Franklin J. Tolby was the catalyst that started the Colfax County War. *Courtesy author's collection.*

William R. Morley, once the chief civil engineer for the Santa Fe Railroad, was editor of the *Cimarron News and Press*. He was also suspected by the Santa Fe Ring as author of some of the inflammatory letters. It is said that Morley aimed to aggravate both the Ring and the settlers in the editorials, which quickly made the newspaperman a target for the Ring. According to an article by Rasch for the *New Mexico Historical Review*, "The People of the Territory of New Mexico VS. The Santa Fe Ring," the letters were penned by Simeon Harrison Newman.

Attacks against Morley and his family began as the postmaster of Cimarron stated that Morley's wife, Ada McPherson Morley, who later became involved in the women's suffrage movement in New Mexico, had "robbed the mails" by removing a letter dropped in the box by her mother. The letter, written to the attorney general of the United States, stated at great length the troubles plaguing Colfax County at the hand of Thomas B. Catron. Ada, not wanting any further trouble, retrieved the letter from the open box, fearing retaliation against her family. No immediate complaint had been filed, and Mrs. Morley denied taking it in the first place. The United States district attorney, Thomas Catron, a leader of the Santa Fe Ring, stated that he intended to use this case to quash Morley's opinions. Ada Morley was indicted on the postal charges, although she was never arrested, due mainly to the interference of the town gunslinger.

The owner of the *Cimarron News and Press*, William R. Morley, was outspoken against the Santa Fe Ring. *Courtesy author's collection.*

When an attempt to arrest Ada Morley was made, Clay Allison intervened. He was quoted as saying, "Bring that woman to trial and not a man will come out of the courtroom alive." A prosecutor was never found for the case, so it did not come to trial. Rasch stated, "Perhaps a more likely version is that Catron requested Marshal John Pratt to defer action because the lady was pregnant, and Postmaster McCulloch finally persuaded him to drop the charges." Allison, a defender of the underdog, may very well have intervened in the manner stated, as his sympathies leaned against the Ring at this point, and the Ring was trying to save face.

Ada McPherson Morley would outlive her husband by thirty-four years, spending twelve of those blind. Her blindness did not prevent Ada from being an activist until the end. She was thought to have written 100 to 150 letters a month and to have made the three-mile hike to the post office to mail them. William R. Morley was taken from her under suspicious circumstances, leading many to believe it was the work of the ever-present Santa Fe Ring.

A group of citizens who lived in the Sugarite Valley, which is about fifty miles northeast of Cimarron, led by the George Coe family, were also being harassed by the Santa Fe Ring. Charges of trespassing against the Coes had been levied by a cattleman who leased land from the Maxwell Land Grant A hearing before Judge Joseph Palen of the Santa Fe Ring was postponed for a third time, causing distress for the Coe family. Clay Allison intervened, to which George Coe was quoted as saying, "When Allison butted in, business started to pick up."

Clay made no bones about the fact the situation "graveled" him. He paid a visit to the plaintiff and told him to move on, the further the better. Then Allison called on Judge Palen to inform him that he would be acting as the Coe's "special attorney." He urged there be no further delays to a hearing. When Palen noticed Clay was in the courtroom armed, he told the gunfighter he had a "good notion to charge Clay Allison with contempt of court." He did not.

The next day, the plaintiff apparently had taken Clay's advice, as he failed to appear, allowing the charges to be dropped against the Coes. This act of defiance was said to have won Clay Allison a "bunch of devoted backers" while driving the thorn deeper in the side of the Santa Fe Ring. Ironically, the Coes eventually moved to Lincoln, in southeastern New Mexico, just in time to be a part of the Lincoln County War and become friends with the outlaw Billy the Kid.

VIGILANTE JUSTICE

Reverend Oscar P. McMains, who took on Reverend Tolby's quest against the Ring, enlisted rancher William Lowe to help him with his quest to expose the truth of the former mail carrier, Cruz Vega, who was the suspected party in Tolby's death, and hopefully get to the bottom of the preacher's murder. The two devised a plan in which Lowe hired Vega to watch a corn stockpile of his behind his barn over the Halloween weekend. Lowe did just that. While Vega and Lowe were seated at a campfire talking, a large group of masked men approached.

One of the masked men, rumored to have been Clay Allison, according to William Lowe's account, said, "Halloo boys" and put a lariat around Vega's neck. The lassoed man was taken by force about five hundred feet to a telegraph pole. The party was deadly silent as several of them climbed the pole, put the rope over the wire and began to raise and lower Vega numerous times, slowly choking him while interrogating him until McMains was satisfied with the information they received.

Said to not have the stomach for violence, which was now mixed with the heavy drinking of the men, Reverend McMains left the group and went to the Poñil Creek Ranch, where he was staying for the night. McMains later stated in a deposition he was not concerned for Vega's fate, since the men appeared too drunk to do any real damage. This thinking proved deadly for Vega, who was found the next morning slumped over at the foot of the telegraph pole, deep rope burns in his neck and a piece of his skull lying nearby caused by an apparent gunshot.

Although the man had begged for his life and denied any wrongdoing, his reputation and that of his family had preceded him, and the mob was not convinced. Clay Allison was not known for his compassion when it came to murderers of innocents. Cruz Vega had been tortured into revealing that he was present when Tolby was killed, but it was Manuel Cardenas who had done the deed.

Vigilante justice prevailed in the New Mexico Territory.

According to an article in the *Livestock Journal of New Mexico*, "Clay Allison, so well-known in Colfax County, is in Las Vegas and on Wednesday, (May 12) said to the reporter of the *Las Vegas Optic* that he wishes emphatically to deny that he is in any sort of sympathy with Oscar P. McMains in his incessant agitation of the Maxwell Land Grant question." This article was written on May 14, 1888, nearly one year after Clay's death.

In the book *Chasing the Santa Fe Ring*, David L. Caffey states that before his death, Vega implicated in Tolby's death not only Manuel Cardenas but also three prominent citizens of Cimarron who were also members of the Santa Fe Ring. Cardenas, learning of this, turned himself in to the sheriff to be protected from an angry lynch mob. Also implicated were the original mail contractor Florencio Donoghue, probate judge Dr. Robert Longwill and attorney Melvin W. Mills. Cardenas stated that these men offered him $500 to rid the Ring of its biggest opponent. Cardenas said he refused the job, so they offered it to Vega, who accepted it. Since Vega was dead, there was no one to deny these allegations.

Due to the accusations of Cardenas and previous actions by Clay Allison, Dr. Longwill fled to Fort Union and then on to Santa Fe for protection while being pursued by Allison's posse. Attorney Mills, hearing of the claims by Cardenas, returned from Santa Fe to face the charges in Cimarron. Donoghue was forced to share a jail cell with Cardenas.

Cruz's uncle Francisco "Pancho" Griego let it be known that he was sworn to avenge his nephew's death by killing Clay. Word of his threat spread like wildfire in the small mining communities. Rumors surfaced later Griego was the perpetrator of the crime, as Tolby had witnessed him shoot a man and threatened to seek an indictment against Griego. Tolby was said to have been silenced to prevent further actions against Griego and to rid the Ring of a thorn—killing two birds with one stone. Tolby's death remains unsolved and is one of the biggest murder mysteries in New Mexico, despite a $3,000 reward offered by none other than the Santa Fe Ring for information leading to solving the murder.

Originally brought to Cimarron as a young man by a rancher known as Boggs, Pancho Griego was tasked with finding workers for the Maxwell Land Grant. Griego wanted married men for colonization. As a native of Santa Fe, Griego served as a deputy sheriff until he started following local badmen. He had several children and was said to have been an excellent shot and horseman. He was known to have been vocal about not liking the attitudes of the Texans who were moving to New Mexico. Griego later remarked that if he could kill the famous Clay Allison, it would bring the rest of the Texans down.

On November 1, 1875, the St. James Hotel was once again the site of violence involving Clay Allison. Pancho Griego confronted Clay in the saloon under the pretense of only wanting to talk with him, but Clay knew Griego had been bragging around the valley he was going to kill the Texas gunfighter. When Griego began to fan himself with his sombrero,

Clay recognized this to be a diversionary tactic used by gunmen and took immediate action, shooting Griego in the chest twice, killing him.

In one bizarre version of this event, which added insult to injury, Clay was reported to have stripped down (which he loved to do), tied a red ribbon around his manhood and danced a jig over the corpse of his unlucky opponent. The entire scene cleared the saloon of any witnesses quickly.

It is then written in several accounts that owner Henri Lambert turned his back, pretending not to have witnessed the events unfolding in front of him and immediately turned off the lanterns as his patrons scattered when the shooting began. Lambert locked up the saloon, not to return until the next morning. It was then Griego's fate was supposedly learned, as he was found slumped over in the corner of the saloon with two red bloodstains trailing down on the wall behind him. Clay was charged with Griego's murder, but the case was dropped. The death was determined to be, as with Clay's other killings, self-defense.

Ironically, by killing Griego, Clay Allison unknowingly avenged the deaths of three Union Buffalo Soldiers Griego had killed previously. Clay's actions were not a surprise to the townsfolk, but the fact Allison left Griego's horse tethered to the hitch in front of Lambert's Inn all night without feed did not win him any popularity contests.

Clay Allison spent a great deal of his time in Cimarron at Henri Lambert's saloon.

Rasch wrote the following:

Warrants were issued by Justice Trauer for the other parties implicated by Cardenas. Mills and Donoghue were promptly arrested, but Longwill eluded a determined pursuit by Allison, his brother John, and Peter Burlinson [sic] and reached Fort Union in safety. At his request the commanding officer dispatched a detachment of troops to Cimarron. En route the party encountered Special Deputy Sheriff John Allison and Burlinson [sic]. The troops refused to permit them to execute their warrants for the arrest of Longwill, but also declined to honor the latter's demands that the two men be taken into custody. Longwill thereupon returned to the fort and then drove to Santa Fe, hotly but futilely pursued by the sheriff of San Miguel County and a posse. Mills, a member of the Territorial Legislature, was discharged for lack of evidence, and eventually the charges against Donoghue and Longwill were quietly dropped.

In the November 9, 1875 issue of the *Weekly New Mexico* in Santa Fe, the following was written: "Friends of [Tolby], particularly his fellow preacher Oscar P. McMains, were convinced Cruz Vega, a part-time postal delivery man who had been seen in the vicinity of [Tolby's] murder, had actually killed the [Methodist] minister. McMains led a masked mob, which allegedly included Allison, grabbed Vega and strung him up to a telegraph pole near the Poñil Creek. [The mob] lifted and lowered Vega until he accused Manuel Cardenas as having killed Tolby."

Attorney Melvin Mills, in Santa Fe at the time filing charges against McMains and Allison for Vega's death, returned to face his own accusations in Cimarron. In a rare change of events, Allison was credited with preventing Mills from being hanged by a vigilante mob as he exited his coach. Clay was fast to boast this fact around town every chance he got, much to Mills's chagrin.

The Ninth Cavalry (Buffalo Soldiers) was dispatched from Fort Union and arrived just in time to stop the proceedings so Mills could be released due to lack of evidence. Charges against Longwill and Donoghue were also later dropped. Cardenas had set the Cimarron rumor mill ablaze when he retracted his earlier statement implicating Mills and Longwill. Many suspected Cardenas had been influenced by the Santa Fe Ring to say he had been forced at gunpoint to accuse these men of the crime by Joseph Herberger, a man who was given political promises by Mills and Longwill. But when they reneged, he sought revenge by setting them up for Tolby's murder with Cardenas's confession.

Ten days after Pancho Griego's death, the authorities arrested Manuel Cardenas and placed him in the Cimarron jail, but once again Reverend McMains was not going to play by the rules. His vigilante group, including Allison, grabbed Cardenas out of the jail and beat him into a confession. During this confession, Cardenas revealed that he and Vega had ambushed Tolby and carried out the killing, paid for by Santa Fe Ring members.

For some unknown reason, the mob allowed Cardenas to go free, but he was rearrested shortly afterward. As the prisoner was being taken back to jail, a tall man dressed in black clothing exited the shadows long enough to shoot Cardenas to death. This shadow figure quickly retreated into the darkness, not to be seen again. The phantom was thought to be Clay Allison.

In the newspaper reporting tone of the time, Cardenas's death was said to "not be a tragedy for anyone," since the man had a poor reputation and had also been recently accused of murder and publicly flogged in the Taos Plaza.

STOP THE PRESSES!

Coeditor of the *Cimarron News and Press*, William R. Morley, father of the author of *No Life for a Lady*, Agnes Morley Cleveland, was exhausted by the antics of Clay Allison in the Cimarron Valley. Allison must have had a permanent slot in the paper for at least five years while he was a cattleman in the region. It is widely written Morley included a scathing editorial reprimanding Allison for his activities and accusing him of being the leader of the vigilante mobs out to avenge the death of Reverend Tolby.

The newspaper suddenly suspended operation in January 1876, when Clay Allison, Joe Curtis and a couple of other Allison supporters walked across the plaza in Cimarron, New Mexico, after spending a great amount of time at Lambert's Inn building up a good amount of anger and forcefully opened the door to the newspaper office with a pole. The group then removed the newspaper's printing press and type trays from the office and dumped them lock, stock and barrel into the Cimarron River in a fit of drunken rage on behalf of the squatters and Clay's indignation.

The group then returned to the office and handwrote on blank pieces of newsprint, "Clay Allison's Edition," and took these to local saloons to sell for twenty-five cents apiece. Despite his criminal proclivities, Clay was said to be well educated, used excellent grammar and diction and could express himself well in writing. Covered in a "goodly amount" of printer's ink, Clay threatened Henri Lambert with harm when Lambert inquired about the

Upset by an article, Allison tossed the *Cimarron News and Press* printing press into the Cimarron River. The author of the article quickly moved. *Courtesy author's collection.*

reason for the ink, saying something might happen to him if he mentioned the occurrence again. Lambert never asked again.

The next morning, when Mrs. Morley, in tears, was assessing the damage to the newspaper office, Clay entered the building. Ada Morley told the gunfighter in no uncertain terms that he should be ashamed of himself for this carnage. Feeling bad, Allison reached into his pocket and reportedly pulled out a roll of money totaling $200 and gave it to the angry woman. Clay told her to buy another press, adding, "I don't fight women." This money was said to have been some of the proceeds from the sale of the "Clay Allison's Edition," which was rumored to have garnered $600 in sales. Clay went on to pledge his total support to the Morleys only if the author of the offending article, Will Dawson, would leave town quickly. Mr. Dawson was seen abruptly leaving Cimarron, reportedly never to return.

Most of the battered press was recovered, allowing the newspaper to resume printing within a few months. For years after, the youth of Cimarron, needing ammunition for their beanshooters, would gather what the locals called the "silent messengers of thought," or individual pieces of print type, which were scattered in the sand along the bottom of the river. Locals say that news type can be found in the Cimarron River to this day. The press would later be moved to the nearby town of Raton, New Mexico, for the establishment of the *Comet* and then the *Raton Range*. William R. Morley would have something in common with the gunfighter when he, too, became a target for assassination by Governor Samuel B. Axtell and the Santa Fe Ring.

The 1870s were described by the January 10, 1907 issue of the *Cimarron News and Press* as "the times which tried men's souls and brought out all the good or all the bad in the character of the individual." This statement was directed toward Clay Allison and his cohorts. Allison was said to have an entourage of forty-five armed men around him during the Colfax County War because there were so many enemies gunning for him.

Clay's largest issue with William Morley was the fact he was a former Union soldier who rode with Sherman during the Civil War. But Allison's hatred for the Ring was so great he eventually forgave Morley's poor judgment and sided with him. Ada McPherson Morley was an accomplished pianist who played for church services. The Morley couple lived in a forty-room mansion owned by Lucien B. Maxwell. The couple had no more trouble with Clay Allison.

Colfax County Ring

Tolby's successor, Reverend Oscar Patrick McMains, took up the "holy war" and formed the Colfax County Ring before his arrest. Newspapers said of the Ring's members that they "rode like avenging angels, cutting down the just and unjust alike." In his public speeches, McMains urged: "Defiance! And contempt for that which is contemptible. The war is on; the precious blood of settlers has been shed, and we must fight it out on this line. No quarter now for the foreign land thieves and their hired assassins."

One can imagine Reverend McMains's fiery speeches also made the Santa Fe Ring uncomfortable, and plans may have been in the works to rid themselves of the newest thorn in their side. McMains's obsession with Tolby's death and the Santa Fe Ring overtook his better judgement; he became the self-appointed commander of the anti-Ring vigilantes, though most knew Clay Allison was really in charge.

The Colfax County Ring consisted of Oscar McMains as chairman and, as vice-presidents, Mathew Lynch, Irwin W. Lacey (whom Clay worked for as a cattle drover), Pete Burleson (known to be Clay's best friend) and S.A. Brown. Frank Springer was secretary. Clay's name was added as a candidate for vice-president, but he asked for it to be withdrawn.

Assassination Attempt

In 1874, Clay was named to the Rules and Regulation Committee on the Maxwell Land Grant as part of the Colfax County Livestock Association. The main purpose of the committee was to prevent homesteaders, of which Clay was one, from occupying grant land. His Vermejo ranch at the convergence of the Vermejo and Red Rivers stretched from Las Animas, Colorado, to French, New Mexico and situated on lands owned by Lucien Maxwell, so the Santa Fe Ring thought it had the cattleman in their back pocket with the commission.

Several of the squatters were accused of shooting cattle on the open range, which infuriated the ranchers of the Santa Fe Ring. The settlers were arrested and brought in for trial, but these trials were repeatedly postponed. Clay Allison, at that time in support of the Santa Fe Ring, was called on for help in getting the settlers off the land. Being a fair man and a person who would stand up for the underdog, Allison reversed his position and backed the accused. This began Clay's first battle with the Santa Fe Ring. It would almost cost him his life, as Governor Axtell called for his assassination.

Clay Allison was not one to back down from a fight or to allow anyone to get the upper hand. He quickly became known as the "Allison problem." William Morley and attorney Frank Springer also began a campaign against the Ring and the governor when it was learned they decided to remove the judiciary of Colfax County to Taos County, some sixty miles away. Citizens of Colfax County would be at the mercy of the Taos juries and ultimately the Ring.

> *"What was done, if anything, by the governor in regard to Colfax County after passage of the act* [attaching Colfax County to Taos for judicial purposes]*?" Investigator Frank W. Angel asked Springer, who replied: "After my interview with Gov. Axtell…I returned to Cimarron and had a meeting with a number of citizens, at which an invitation was prepared, directed to the governor…requesting him to visit Colfax County.…This was signed by…some 10 or 12* [citizens]. *I mailed it to the governor, who received it, as I afterwards learned, but he never made any direct reply."*

Robert Clay Allison was one of these citizens, which made him an even larger target for the corrupt Santa Fe Ring. An assassination plot by Axtell, Stevens, Longwill and Mills to rid the Ring of any who opposed them was revealed. Any resistance, perceived or otherwise, would be met with gunfire and death.

Axtell's leaked 1876 letters to Ring member Ben Stevens would shine a light on the corruption in the government, especially of Axtell. Frank Springer was told by Ben Stevens, a ringleader and Second Judicial District attorney, he was going to Cimarron to tell the citizens he was trying to entice the governor to pay the town a visit in light of the violent actions that had recently taken place.

Stevens then went to nearby Fort Union and returned with thirty members of L Company of the Ninth Cavalry (Buffalo Soldiers) under Captain Francis Moore with a telegram in hand from Axtell stating, "Do not let it be known that I will be at Cimarron on Saturday's coach." The telegram was brought as proof of Axtell's intentions.

> *Dear Ben—I do not think your definite business is suspected.…*[Colonel Edward] *Hatch* [commander of the military department] *says their opinion is that you weakened and do not want to arrest the man. Have your men placed to arrest him and to kill all the men who resist you or stand with those who do* [not] *resist you. Our man signed the invitation with*

others who were at that meeting for me to visit Colfax—Porter, Morley, Springer, et al....Do not hesitate at extreme measures. Your honor is at stake now, and a failure is fatal.—Yours, etc., S.B. Axtell

In a federal deposition for the trial against Axtell, Frank Springer stated to investigator Frank W. Angel:

The person referred to as "our man," as I afterwards learned from the commander of the troops—was Mr. R.C. Allison. He was not under indictment for anything, nor was there any charge known to be pending against him. He occupied a prominent place in the eyes of the public on account of his well-known desperate courage and resolute character....He was one of the signers of the invitation to the governor and was a perfect guaranty of courteous treatment on his part, as Allison was known to be keenly scrupulous in such matters....If he had come to the coach upon the invitation of the governor...and had found himself beset with soldiers seeking to arrest him, his first motion would have been one of resistance; in that case, according to the instructions of Gov. Axtell, not only he, but those who stood with him, were to be killed....

[I was convinced] *that the arrest of Allison was not the real object of the expedition. If it had been, it could easily have been done in a straightforward manner...and there would have been no necessity for the significant coupling of the names of Messrs. Porter, Morley and myself, with suggestions to kill...those who resisted.*

Trust of the governor did not run deep with the citizens of Cimarron, especially those mentioned in the invitation. None of the men met Axtell's coach when it arrived, thus thwarting the murderous plans of the governor. Learning of Axtell placing a price on his head, Clay devised a plan that could be termed either foolhardy or heroic, depending on the outcome. Some historians record Allison intercepted Axtell's coach on its way back to Taos just to chat. It is also believed Allison and Axtell came to an agreement of sorts during this fifty-mile journey and Clay made his own way back home. We will never know what deal was made, but one could bet Allison got the upper hand.

In any case, the situation remained so volatile soldiers from Fort Union remained in Cimarron after Axtell reportedly left. It was during this time that Clay's friend Davy Crockett became the town bully and began raising Cain with cohort Gus Heffron at local watering holes. Crockett, having

HENRI LAMBERT

Top: Henri Lambert was a personal chef of both Presidents Abraham Lincoln and Ulysses S. Grant.

Bottom: Members of the Ninth Cavalry Regiment (Buffalo Soldiers) were stationed at Fort Union.

been raised near Allison in Tennessee, was of the same mindset as Allison about the Black Ninth Cavalry Buffalo Soldiers.

As the two troublemakers made their rounds, they decided to visit Lambert's Inn (now the St. James Hotel) for one last nightcap. After spending time at the saloon, Crockett attempted to leave but was prevented by someone who was trying to come inside. This person was a soldier from the Ninth Cavalry. Crockett promptly shot and killed him in a rage. To add insult to injury, Crockett went on to turn his attention to three other soldiers seated at a card table, killing two of them. Heffron and Crockett fled town on foot, as their horses were stabled where the soldiers were camped.

The Ninth's commanding officer, Captain Moore, had previously asked saloon owners not to serve his troops and ordered the troops to stay away from the town businesses when they arrived. But his orders were ignored, resulting in the deaths. Racism was still a real issue with the Texans, even though the Civil War had long since ended.

Remaining at large for several months after the incident, Crockett plotted with a sympathetic justice of the peace for leniency before turning himself in to face the charges for the murders of the soldiers. Appearing before the justice of the peace, Crockett claimed that he was drunk at the time and therefore could not be held responsible. The court agreed, and Crockett was acquitted of murder. This hothead was said to hold the opinion that "putting uniforms on former slaves was adding insult to injury." He showed no remorse for his actions. Crockett was fined fifty dollars and court costs for a reduced charge of carrying a firearm.

Thinking his acquittal gave him free range, reportedly Crockett's actions became insufferable to the citizens of Cimarron. Author Leon Metz writes that the pair "terrorized Cimarron's peaceful population with sporadic gunshots, rambunctious behavior, and brazen threats." This led to Crockett riding his horse into a building on one occasion, shooting into the ceiling and forcing the occupants to perform demeaning services for him such as shining his boots.

GOVERNOR SAMUEL BEACH AXTELL

The mention of Clay Allison must have sent bolts of lightning down Governor Axtell's spine, as the gunfighter was a huge thorn in the state leader's side. The violence perpetrated by Allison in Colfax County was legendary and, in the opinion of many, out of control. After hearing of the lynching of Cruz Vega, Axtell put a $100 bounty on Allison's head and slated the gunfighter and two others for assassination. These actions would land Axtell in hot water.

Between 1851 and statehood in 1912, the New Mexico Territory endured eighteen presidentially appointed territorial governors; the people were left without a choice or voice. It is written that this led to chaos and that "corruption had become so ingrained that a 'no-party pattern' of politics had developed. This meant that instead of being governed by a single political party or the democratic ideal of two parties, a coalition of local interests, regardless of party differences, controlled territorial government." Samuel Beach Axtell, the ninth appointed governor, proved to be the most unpopular in the territory, mostly at his own hand.

Born in Ohio to a farming household, Axtell could trace his roots to the Revolutionary War and the War of 1812. Appointed governor of the New Mexico Territory by President Ulysses S. Grant in 1875 after the death of the sitting governor, Marsh Giddings, Axtell was accused of profiting from the Mountain Meadows Massacre in 1857 while serving as a district attorney in California and was not well liked in Utah, where he had previously been appointed governor. A Salt Lake newspaper editorialized Axtell's removal from Utah this way: "We have not yet heard of a single instance of regret at this parasite's removal. He came here trusted; he has betrayed that trust and will take his departure despised and disgraced.... [W]e cannot but rejoice at the interposition which caused the noxious weed to be transplanted to the soil of Mexico."

Special Agent of the Department of the Interior Frank Warner Angel described Axtell in a notebook: "Conceited. Egotistical easily flattered tool unwittingly of the ring—goes off 'half-cocked'." Samuel Axtell was not a well-liked man in Utah or in the New Mexico Territory.

Controversy followed Axtell like a shadow throughout his political career, including accusations of his being a bishop in the Latter-day Saints. According to New Mexico author Don Bullis, he conspired with the New Mexico Indian tribes to wipe out the "gentile population" of the territory so that "a Kingdom of Mormon could be set up" in the territory. Axtell was also linked, indirectly, to the corrupt actions of the Santa Fe Ring.

5

A MAN AND HIS HORSE

A Love Story

With the introduction of the horse into North America by Spanish explorer Hernán Cortés in 1519, this mighty steed became a staple in the lives of residents of America. Without a horse in the West, life was extremely difficult, if not downright impossible. Horses were the only means of transportation available to many inhabitants. A strong bond has developed between man and horse since then in the West; each needed the other to survive.

Allison's horses were as much a part of his personality as was his weapon of choice. He was famous for owning some of the best examples of horseflesh in the West and enjoyed horses that were either black or white in color. He made a striking impression when he rode into town—besides the fear he already instilled. Often described as extremely handsome, Clay Allison was a showman and enjoyed the attention he received. And he was always scheming.

Norman B. Wiltsey described Clay Allison in this manner: "Clay rode on his cream white 'warhorse,' dressed all in black and white, with his jet mustache a-curl. Six feet two inches in height, slim-hipped, wide-shouldered, with flashing blue eyes. Allison could have made any of today's cowboy film stars take a back seat when it came to good looks and dramatic appearance. In addition to being a screwball, he was a terrific ham and as inordinately vain as a chorus girl."

Interestingly, author F. Stanley described Allison in a different manner.

> *Clay Allison had a Roman nose, square set face, large boned and was blonde with a mustache worn long, which drooped below his chin, and his right eye was slightly crossed so that the iris seemed to be just off the bridge of the nose. Ears were large, stuck out from his face a little which he could conceal somewhat with his long curly hairs (center parted). Upper lip thin, did not curve at the corners which gave an impression of a rather large mouth. Lower lip thick and protruded a bit causing a shadow to appear at times over his firm round chin. He wore expensive clothes, usually in fashion and never missed buying a shirt every time he was in town. He wore a sixteen neck.*

Clay had a healthy respect for the horses he owned and treated them kindly. You might think, given his military background, that he may have had a harsh hand when it came to animals, but it was quite the opposite. Being from Tennessee, he was exposed to the well-bred equines available to those who had the money to acquire them. Allison's appreciation was high for horses, especially if they were fast. Exceedingly competitive, he loved to race his horses, expecting to win every time. Newspapers of the time were quick to mention the snow-white or black horse Clay was riding whenever his episodes proved newsworthy.

RAVEN THE PACER

A story about Clay's most beloved horse comes from a lengthy December 24, 1883 article printed in, ironically, the *Tennessean*. Sounding much like the treasured 1877 children's book *Black Beauty* by English author Anna Sewell, the story of Black Raven is equally as heartbreaking. It is not known exactly when Clay acquired his version of Black Beauty, but Raven is said to have been a showstopper and head-turner. The dashing, dark-haired outlaw on his gleaming black mount must have been a sight to behold. If Clay's reputation had not preceded him, this display of confidence would have been cause for caution for anyone thinking of challenging the gunfighter.

Raven played a role in Clay's desire to be the best at everything. This horse and Clay were inseparable, "almost as inseparable as the Siamese twins," and Raven was highly trained. Many accounts have been written of Allison not tethering Raven to a hitching post in town but allowing him to graze freely.

A likeness of what Clay Allison's favorite horse, Raven, may have looked like.

Whenever his owner needed him, a whistle was all it took to bring the steed to him at full speed. The article noted Raven was known as an excellent race horse and won races from the panhandle of Texas to Colorado.

The heartbreaking story tells of a broken, spavined black horse attempting to pull a heavy cart in the streets of Denver, Colorado. An older gentleman called out to the animal by name. The formerly gleaming black gelding immediately turned his weary head toward the man, and it was clear he recognized the voice as he moved in haste toward the man.

Black Raven first made his appearance in the West along in the 60's as a pacer. His first races were won in the Panhandle of Texas, when $10,000 was not considered an unusually large stake, when the wires, strung with purses of gold were the stakeholders, and the revolver as judge in case of difficulty. Black Raven never was beaten; not a horse in the West could catch him and he reigned as king of the turf until a change in his career occurred.

His owner after leaving Texas made a tour of New Mexico and Colorado, scooping in money wherever he went and becoming the envied of all men because he owned such a horse. Among the men who cast a cautious eye on Raven was Clay Allison, who was known as a very dangerous man and who, with his brother John Allison, owned large cattle ranches in Southern Colorado and Northern New Mexico.

Allison made the acquaintance of the owner and succeeded in buying the animal at a good price. From that day Clay Allison and his big black horse became almost as inseparable as the Siamese twins. They often slept together, and the danger of one was shared by the other. An understanding sprung up between the two and it is known that one saved the life of the other on more than one occasion. Raven was an excellent saddle horse, as he had always been raced under the saddle. Sulkies were unknown in the West in those days.

Clay Allison was a true western character. He was a cattle man and made much money. He was thoroughly imbued with the Western idea of liberty and freedom, and often in his revels committed excesses which placed his life in jeopardy. But he paid for all damages done and escaped injury. He never thirsted for human blood and was not an assassin. That he was called a desperado was because he killed several men who had tried to infringe upon his rights, and even then, he never took advantage of a man. Fair play was his motto and that he always escaped so luckily was because he had more nerve and could shoot quicker and faster than any man in the Territories. In some respects, he was a nobleman in the rough. His adventures would fill volumes.

His reputation as a hard man made many enemies for him. All the desperate characters and man-killers were in awe of him, although bragging of their ability to successfully cope with him. Allison and Raven were horrid specters in their eyes, and they hoped to drive "them away only by foul means." Among the men desirous of "damning" Allison was the Sheriff of Bent County, in this State [Colorado], whose headquarters were at West Las Animas. Allison had frequently visited the town, and although he had injured no one, he was so much feared he generally had things his own way and on more than one occasion he had rode Black Raven into a saloon, made everyone drink, and then shot out the lights for amusement. He was never interfered with, for the simple reason that everyone feared his pistols would bark.

The author of the article mentioned how sad it was to see such a magnificent animal and friend to Clay Allison in such a deplorable condition.

"Raven whinnied with delight at his having met an old acquaintance, and the joy of his brute nature was shining out of his big, luminous eyes. Then he rubbed his nose against the man's shoulder for sympathy, as if saying: 'I haven't always been in this plight, have I?' The gentleman asked the driver a few questions, rubbed the horse's nose and they slowly walked on."

At the conclusion of the article, Black Raven's heartbreaking story is conveyed. The author states that Allison suffered misfortune, which overtook him, and he was "compelled to give up everything he had. The last to go was his old friend, Raven, who was sold under the hammer and in time sent to this city [Denver]. Black Raven is now hauling garbage for his daily allotment of oats. How the mighty have fallen."

In the memoirs of New Mexico territorial governor Miguel Otero, he is proud to tell of the good relationship his family had with Clay Allison—so good, in fact, Otero writes, that the gunfighter once offered ownership of Raven to the senior Otero. The gentleman politely declined but was extremely flattered by the gesture. The Otero family owned a mercantile store in the small town of Otero, near where Clay had his ranch.

It is hoped that this version of the life story of the outstanding Black Raven is completely sensationalized and fictional.

A Beer for My Horse

It was no secret Clay Allison loved his whiskey and beer. Raven, on the other hand, was not so enamored with the liquids. His owner was known to buy his steed a bucket of beer or a bucket of water mixed with whiskey so that Raven could enjoy himself as much as his owner. Whenever Raven was given the liquid, he would sniff it, taste it and then "accidently" tip the bucket over. Raven was an extremely intelligent animal. If a human refused Allison's offer, they would most likely not be around long thereafter.

Raven was much luckier than a horse in the nearby sin city of Loma Parda. As a raucous town which catered to soldiers and outlaws, the local dance hall was the site of many horrific events. One being a drunken outlaw who rode along the street in front of a brothel, scooped up one of the ladies and proceeded to ride into the dance hall without a care. He demanded whiskey for himself, his lady fair and his horse. When the horse refused the drink, the outlaw shot the poor animal in the head and left him lying on the dance hall floor.

Whiskey Peddler

Las Animas, Colorado, was the site of many of the Allisons' antics, as a whiskey salesmen known only as Riggs would find out. Clay and John were well into their cups, so much so that saloon owners locked their doors to protect the few light fixtures they had left.

Riggs's encounter with Clay Allison one day would be one he would not soon forget. While Riggs was crossing the street from the train station to the hotel, a spectacular black horse caught his attention. Greeting the rider, Riggs stated, "That's a mighty fine horse you're riding." To which the rider replied: "Yes, you can bet your life this horse is a fine one. If I say the word, he will kick your hat off. Come over and see."

Taken aback by this remark, recognizing the rider and realizing the man was drunk, Riggs had to think quickly. "Clay, I'll just take your word about the horse kicking off my hat, but I know a better stunt than that. Come and join me in a good drink." Clay questioned this statement and asked, "Riggs, you are not going to break into one of the saloons and commit burglary, are you? You can't get into a saloon any other way with me." To which Riggs said, "I know a better way than that. Tie up your horse and come with me. I'll leave my valise in the drug store until we come back." With Allison's approval, Riggs knocked on the back door of one of the saloons. When there was no answer, he yelled that he was the whiskey salesman. To this, the owner opened the door to a surprise. Riggs stepped into the bar with Allison in tow. A hush fell over the room.

Riggs told the crowd he met Clay Allison and invited him for a drink. Riggs went on to say, "It's my treat, boys; so, let every man in the room take a drink with me to the health, happiness, and long life of Clay Allison." Handing the bartender a five-dollar bill, Riggs told the stunned bartender he could give him the change when he returned from the drugstore with his valise. Of course, Riggs was not seen again in the saloon—for he was on the opposite bound train. The whiskey peddler's popularity took a huge hit that day. He knew he was most likely not welcome back in town after this stunt, but he lived to tell the tale.

6

THE SHOOTIST

Gentleman Killer

I have never shot a man who didn't need killing.
—*Clay Allison*

Fearless and Quick.
—*Lance Robbins*

Don Quixote of the Six-Shooter.
—*J. Frank Dobie*

Fear and survival ran together in the Old West. No matter what your walk of life, the possibility of having to defend yourself at one point or another was always present. Lawlessness, corruption and greed were the mainstays of western society in the 1800s, especially in New Mexico.

Clay Allison has not garnered the same attention of other well-known gunfighters of New Mexico, but he was every bit as dangerous and could hold his ground against any of them when given the opportunity. He was proud to say that he was not a gunman, but a shootist, a word he coined. Clay was not one to start a gunfight on most occasions, but he was always the first to finish a conflict. Quick-tempered, Clay did not wait around for excuses or for someone else to get the jump on him. He acted quickly and with deadly accuracy. The term *gunman* implies sneakiness and murder. To Clay, a gunfighter was chivalrous, generous and sportsmanlike, forced to kill only by circumstances, not by desire.

F. Stanley wrote an accurate review of Clay Allison's character for those times: "Clay Allison was a gunfighter, actually, he became a stockman with the ability to kill, which is a little different than saying he killed for the sake of killing."

Brutal in his split-second decisions, Allison would read a situation and act immediately. He was cunning enough to see the writing on the wall with complete clarity. Allison was known for his deadly accuracy, which was connected to intuition. But he was not known for being a quick draw. This made Clay dangerous. He was ready to pull the trigger without a second thought, usually to the great surprise of the person on the other end of one of his ever-present Colt revolvers.

How Many Did He Kill?

From the beginning of Clay Allison's career, the question of how many people he killed popped up constantly, with answers of varying degrees of accuracy. According to Clay Allison's great-great-nephew Gerry Clay Allison, a descendant of Jesse Allison, Clay's eldest brother, Clay stated himself that he killed eight people. Gerry Allison also claims that Bat Masterson wrote that Clay had killed fifty-six men and was "the best eradicator of badmen, liars, cheats and thieves." Although Bat's statement is possibly more accurate, the large number cited is highly doubtful. An article by Norman Wiltsey states that Clay boasted to Wyatt Earp in their encounter that he had killed twenty-one men, six of them lawmen.

Like the young New Mexico outlaw William H. Bonney, known as Billy the Kid, Clay is given credit in other articles for killing at least twenty-one men, but barring his actions in the Civil War, I believe Clay's number could be a bit lower. According to the records kept by hotel owner Henri Lambert, Allison is credited with ten deaths at the St. James Hotel alone.

In 1872, Lambert had Clay shooting Tom Sunday. Not much is known about this encounter, as the only person to document the killing was Lambert. Then, in 1873, Allison was said to have been involved in two additional killings—the deaths of John Black and Charles Cooper were added to the long list for the gunslinger.

Another rumor states that, in true Clay Allison form, he tried to force everyone in a saloon to drink with him, including a stranger. This stranger was thought to be none other than Jesse James. James refused the demand, and Clay was wise enough to back down. His keen senses told him this man was not going to play his games. Those senses saved his life on many occasions.

Gunfights
St. James Hotel Bar

1872
Clay Allison shot Tom Sunday
Chunk Colbert shot C. Morris
Walleye Henderson shot Pomeroy Laughlin
Walleye Henderson shot Jim Davis

1873
Posse shot Leliciano Butarus (outside)
Clay Allison shot John Black
Clay Allison shot B. Cooper
Henri Lambert killed J. Garcia

1874
Clay Allison shot Frank Harris

1875
Clay Allison killed Manuel Cardenas
Clay Allison killed 5 black Soldiers
Francisco "Pancho" Griego killed 3 black Soldiers
Clay Allison shot Francisco "Pancho" Griego
Davey Crocket II shot Juan Borrego

1876
Gus Heffron, Davey Crocket II killed 3 black Soldiers

1881
Joe McCurdy killed John Stewart

1882
Bob Ford killed Bill Curren

1884
"Prairie Dog" Payne shot Frank Shook
Henri Lambert killed Thomas Rodriguez

Left: A historical list compiled by the staff of the St. James Hotel shows Clay Allison responsible for many of the killings on the site. *Courtesy author's collection.*

Below: Despite causing havoc, Robert Clay Allison is a favorite son of Cimarron, New Mexico.

Clay Allison

Robert Clay Allison (1841-1887) grew up in Tennessee and fought for the Confederate army during the Civil War. After the war he moved to Texas and, in 1866, worked as a drover for John Dawson, Charles Goodnight, and Oliver Loving during their famed cattle drive that passed near Cimarron. By 1872, Allison owned his own ranch ten miles north of town. Soon, Allison's drunken mood swings earned him a reputation as a dangerous man and a gunslinger.

In 1875, local Methodist minister Franklin J. Tolby vocally opposed the new owners of the Maxwell Land Grant. The discovery of Tolby's bullet-ridden body in Cimarron Canyon sparked the Colfax County War during which suspect Francisco Griego was gunned down by Allison in Lambert's Saloon. Griego was one of 20 men Allison is said to have killed during his lifetime. Allison died on July 1, 1887, after falling off a freight wagon. He is buried in Pecos, Texas, under a grave marker that reads: "He never killed a man that did not need killing."

This image of the St. James Hotel ca. 1890 shows the hotel shortly after Henri Lambert had the original one-story saloon expanded but before a balcony seen in later photographs was added. Henri, his wife and four young sons appear in the entrance.

What follows are accounts of some of the men most influential in Clay Allison's gunfighting career. Each saw a varying degree of success against this self-proclaimed shootist.

MASON T. BOWMAN

Shortly after setting up his Vermejo ranch near Cimarron in Colfax County, New Mexico, in the early 1870s, Clay was proud and confident of his skills as a fighter, be it with knives or guns. His reputation was known to all, and he was feared by the smart ones. During this time, Allison had developed a habit of hard drinking and carousing, mainly with his brother John. Clay once had to break John out of a Las Vegas, New Mexico jail, reportedly killing two men and wounding several others in the 1870 incident.

During some of these binges, Clay forced other bar patrons to participate in "quick draw" contests with him. In 1872, Clay was well into his cups when he entered a bar in West Las Animas. Twirling his revolver on his trigger finger, Clay announced that he was Clay Allison and "I want every son-of-a-gun to take off his hat here." Although most of the men did as Clay said, he found one person was not afraid to stand up to the supposed man-killer: Mason T. "Mace" Bowman, a former sheriff and deputy sheriff of Colfax County. Bowman rendered the bar silent as he boldly said, "All the Allisons that ever came from Tennessee couldn't make him take his hat off."

Clay slowly looked over the pale, glum-looking man and decided, "Well, take a drink with your hat on, then." As everyone started to drink again, Allison proposed the following to Mace Bowman:

> *This yere small State ain't big enough for two such men as you an' me; our trail are always crossin' an' one of us oughter moved a good while back. Now, I'll tell you how we'll fix it. We'll put our guns on the bar and get over to the other side of the room. One of the boys will give the word and the man who gets his gun first is goin' to play in big luck, an' the other won't be near so numerous around this dance hall tomorrow raisin' disputes an' making bad blood among good, quiet people.*

Bowman and Allison knew each other's capabilities and that if one of them got the drop on the other, the slower man would surely die. There was no trust between the gunfighters, and each was extremely leery of the other. Bowman was a deadly fast gunslinger, and he knew he could outdraw the cocky Allison.

The quickest draw was Bowman, who startled not only Allison but also the saloon girl who was sweet on Clay. She demanded a gun to shoot Bowman if he followed through, even though the weapons were empty. Allison gathered his thoughts and said, "You're the best man, Bowman, this is a fair fight." To which Bowman replied: "If I didn't know I was the best man, I'd drill you right now while it's my way, but I don't have to kill a man with his woman looking on. So, we'll quit right here, but don't come bulgin' around me no more."

The *El Dorado Republican* of El Dorado, Kansas, stated in an article on May 17, 1889 (two years after Clay's death), that a round of drinks was bought, ending the incident. Allison later said Bowman was the one who taught him the most, especially the unusual way of drawing a gun.

After the killing of Pancho Griego, Clay Allison was a wanted man. Mace Bowman was the sheriff at the time and sought to take Clay in for the death. In another rendition of the story, according to author-historian J. Frank Dobie, "being arrested was against Allison's principles, so of course he resisted." Clay, ever quick with a scheme, decided the two men would put their weapons on the bar at Lambert's Inn, walk twenty-five steps and shoot. The fact that Clay is said to have had a pronounced limp from having shot himself in the foot has made historians wonder why he would agree to a slow footrace, especially against Mace Bowman.

Harsh words were spoken between Allison and Bowman when Allison was well into his cups. Allison supposedly said that he should kill Bowman right there. The words were not recorded, but it is said that Bowman stepped back from the bar and told Allison to "have at it." To which Clay, although inebriated, said with regret in his voice, "Hell. No use in us both dying," and walked out of the saloon. In another version, Clay was the quickest and leveled his pistol at Mace's puffed-up chest. Bowman struck his own chest with his fist, taunting Allison, "Shoot, you son of a gun." Clay held steady but replied, "Mace, you are too brave a man to kill." The men shook hands, and the attempted arrest was forgotten.

CHUNK COLBERT

On January 7, 1874, a boastful gunman by the name of Chunk Colbert (also recorded as Tolbert) met his match at the Clifton House in Colfax County, New Mexico. Colbert came to the house after he heard Allison might be there and to start trouble. Bragging seven notches on his weapon from the men he had killed and itching to add an eighth with Allison, Colbert was playing with fire. (It was later known that Colbert had only one confirmed kill to his name, Charles Morris in Cimarron, New Mexico, who Colbert claimed was trying to steal his wife.) Word of these bold claims quickly reached Clay, who everyone knew was not one to back down from a challenge.

Chunk Colbert, sometimes known as Chubbs, was, it turns out, the nephew of (Frank) Zachary Colbert, the ferryman mentioned earlier who Allison had beaten senseless nine years before. Apparently, Colbert had never forgotten and was ready to settle the score. There was obviously no trust between the two men, as Colbert thought himself clever and coy, much smarter than this Tennessee farm boy.

Two versions of the ensuing events have been presented by historians. One has it Colbert confronted Clay and the two men decided on a duel after running a few horse races. In another, Clay cunningly went by the adage "keep your friends close and your enemies closer" and pretended to be unaware of Colbert's threats while playing along with the braggart's plan. Certainly, both versions could be true.

Another story has Chunk buying a beautiful sorrel from Tom Stockton, the owner of Clifton House, and bragging it was the fastest horse in the West. Clay Allison, always ready for competition, placed a twenty-dollar gold piece and a five-dollar bill as a wager against this claim. Clay told Chunk if he could make the bet, they would have a race. The racetrack was a quarter-mile-long straight line, and two Englishmen staying at the Clifton House were quickly appointed as judges. Wisely, the judges deemed the race a tie to avoid bloodshed—including their own.

After Clay's horse, Raven, succeeded in beating Colbert's Thoroughbred, the men decided to break bread at the Clifton House. (Accounts by J. Frank Dobie in his 1942 article "Clay Allison, 'Gentleman Killer' of the West, Specialized in Unusual Killings" and Maurice G. Fulton in his *Southwest Review* article have Raven losing, thus angering Clay, as it gave Chunk bragging rights.) A dramatic newspaper account had the men sitting across from each other, slowly stirring cups of coffee with the barrels of their guns as they sized each other up for upward of two hours. It took two hands to pour the coffee from the carafes; Clay refused to pour, since he knew Chunk was gunning for him.

When the meal arrived, Clay placed his pistol beside his soup bowl, and Chunk placed his weapon in his lap, both wanting to have quick access if needed. Partway through the meal, Colbert chose this time to attempt to draw his weapon from underneath the table and get a jump on Allison. Unfortunately for Colbert, the barrel caught on the corner of the table, sending the shot astray and narrowly missing Clay's head. Being nimble and perceptive, Clay was able to avoid the bullet while drawing his weapon from

Clay Allison shot Chunk Colbert and continued with his meal with the dead man sitting across from him with his head in the soup bowl.

the tabletop. The red circle in the center of Colbert's forehead provided proof that Clay was a better shot.

Much to the horror of the other diners, Colbert's head fell forward and landed square in his soup bowl. Any attempts by the diners to leave were met with ire from Clay, so everyone remained until he finished his meal and left the dining room. After leaving the Clifton House, it is said Clay rang a bell located on the porch and announced the "festivities to happen later are cancelled due to the illness of one of the parties." This statement led some to believe a shootout had been planned between the men.

One of Clay Allison's most famous quotes arose from this occurrence. When asked why he would accept a dinner invitation from a man who clearly was gunning for him, Clay replied, "Because I didn't want to send a man to hell on an empty stomach." In Miguel Otero's statement of this event, he insinuates that it was Chunk who first spoke this famous quote.

Another account given of this horrific incident, by Clay's close friend and former governor of the New Mexico Territory Miguel Otero, told of the two men, after drinking together heavily, devising a scheme which sounded like a true Allison plot. In this plan, the enemies would face each other on horseback at one hundred yards, then race at full speed toward each other, shooting along the way. The man left in the saddle would obviously be the victor. In this version, they were saved by the bell—the dinner bell, to be exact. Either way, the rest, as they say, is history.

Colbert was buried behind the Clifton House in an unmarked grave. Knowing the importance of a Christian burial service, Clay insisted a

Nothing but a sign remains of the Clifton House, site of many a horse race. *Courtesy author's collection.*

preacher give Colbert a proper sendoff. When none could be found, he enlisted Bill Robinson, a young man who happened to be carrying an Episcopal prayer book. He agreed to read a few words at the poor man's grave, but this was agreed to only if the words *parson* or *preacher* were not attached to him, since he was new to the country and did not want to be known as such.

Clay said: "Friends, mourners and others. Bill Robinson here is going to give the late Chuck Colbert a decent Christian burial. This is on condition, however, that nobody will ever allude to him as Parson, Preacher, or any other such name. Now I want you all to understand this, and to realize that I am under obligation to see that his request is complied with." Nobody ever violated this request.

The passage of time has taken away both the Clifton House due to fire and the knowledge of the location of the gunman's grave. In a side note, Colbert's friend Charles Cooper was later seen riding beside Clay Allison leaving the area after the previous events. January 19, 1874, would be the last time Cooper was seen alive. Clay was later arrested under the suspicion of murder, but he was released due to lack of evidence. The fate of Charles Cooper is still unknown, and this incident would come back to haunt Clay.

According to an 1883 article, Sheriff Pete Burleson was ordered by the district judge to issue a warrant for Clay's arrest. Although Burleson and Allison were the best of friends, Pete was cautious in the delivery of the warrant to his friend. "I have an order for your arrest and am ordered to take you into court at once." To which Clay responded, "All right, I'll go with you." The next statement was one the sheriff feared most in saying: "I'll have to disarm you. Give me your guns." Clay's frown was said to have made Burleson tremble. Clay responded: "No, I'll go with you, but no man can have my revolvers. I'll not be taken at a disadvantage. I'll go peacefully, but don't ask too much of me." Pete saw no reason to push his friend and endanger his life, so his prisoner was allowed to remain armed.

As Burleson brought Allison into the courtroom, the judge ordered the prisoner be disarmed. To which Pete declared: "I am compelled to disobey the order. If the Court or any other man wants to disarm the prisoner, he can try it. I want none of it in mine."

Clay spoke up. "There's no necessity for all this trouble. I came here peacefully. I haven't resisted anyone, and I want a trial. But I warn you all not to go too far. These revolvers are mine, and I intend to keep them. Don't go too far with me."

The judge landed his gavel and stated, "Mr. Bailiff, adjourn this court without date." The bailiff yelled, "Hear, ye! Hear ye!," and the courtroom was emptied, including Allison. After his scrape with the law, Clay returned to his beloved Raven, who rubbed noses with him in congratulations. Allison was tried for the killing of Chunk Colbert, but it was ruled self-defense. A law in 1884 loosely stated that if your opponent is wearing a weapon, whether he can use it or not, and you get the drop on him, it is deemed self-defense, since the other person is armed. This ruling would lead to many deaths.

MARION LITTRELL

Known as a self-made man, Marion Littrell began herding cattle in 1869. This brought him to New Mexico from Texas to work for eleven years with the Maxwell Company. Littrell oversaw twenty-five thousand head of Maxwell cattle at any given time.

As the foreman for the Maxwell Land Grant and Railway Company, a Colfax County sheriff, a vocal supporter of the Union and the future husband of one of Clay Allison's love interests, Carrie Gale Sexton, Marion Littrell had no fear of the notorious gunfighter and was thought to have bested Allison at the draw on one occasion. Legend has it that Marion was twice as fast in unholstering his weapon than Clay, so Clay was extremely lucky to have survived the encounter. Allison did not go up against Littrell again.

G.W. "Cap" Arrington

An interesting character himself, George Washington Arrington was born John C. Orrick Jr. in Greensboro, Alabama. After losing his father in 1848 and his stepfather, who was killed in the Civil War, in 1861, Orrick enlisted in the Confederate army and rode with John S. Mosby's guerrillas at the age of sixteen. Like Clay Allison, Orrick worked as a spy for the Confederates. Orrick then went to Mexico to join Emperor Maximilian's army as a mercenary, but his timing was off, so he returned to Alabama. There, the young warrior murdered a Black businessman in Greensboro in 1867 before going to Central America and then to Texas in 1870.

It was in Texas that he took the name George Washington Arrington to mask his criminal past. He went to work for the Texas Central Railway in Houston. He later hired on as a cowboy to run a herd to Brown County. It was there that Arrington enlisted in the Frontier Battalion of Texas Rangers. His work was recognized as distinguished in his efforts tracking outlaws and fugitives. Arrington was the third man to give Allison a cause for caution, and Clay left the dangerous Texas Ranger alone.

In his obituary, Arrington was said to have been "fearless and could track outlaws and bring them to court when others lost the trail. He was one of the few men who Clay Allison, a notorious gunman and 'killer,' respected as his equal in nerve and quick action." Clay may have been afraid that Arrington would aggravate his allergy to being arrested in his encounters with the man in Mobeetie and Hemphill.

Union Soldiers

The Civil War never ended for Clay Allison. He had selective memory with a few northern soldiers and sympathizers (like Henri Lambert, who had supported the North), but for the most part Allison was brutal in his actions against such persons. One incident occurred after a long day of drinking at the Maxwell House in Cimarron, which was a gambling den and saloon, Clay would move the festivities across the street to Lambert's Inn.

Witnesses reported that Allison was drinking a pint of whiskey every half hour and by this point was extremely drunk. Pensive and stewing in his own thoughts and memories, Clay was in a terrible mood. When five Union soldiers entered the saloon, they observed the man at the bar wearing a Confederate hat. To be polite, they asked if they were welcome there.

Before an answer could be formed, Clay had shot the sergeant in the head, killing him instantly. The other four scattered but were picked off one by one by the drunk gunslinger. When the chaos ended, Clay jammed the bottle of whiskey in his pocket, stepped over his last victim and continued his drinking spree. The soldiers had been unarmed; regulations required they leave their weapons on their horses before entering a drinking establishment.

Although an arrest attempt was made, Clay was never charged for this horrendous act.

LAST GUNFIGHT: MARSHAL CHARLES FABER

Clay Allison's last known killing was recorded in Las Animas, Colorado, on December 21, 1876, at the Olympic Dance Hall. Just before Christmas and at the end of a long cattle drive, Clay and his brother John were in a festive mood. The brothers were known for their ability to raise Cain in every town they visited, and Las Animas was no different. Clay was said to have been a conspicuous figure in the rowdy town, participating in fistfights with rival stock buyers on many occasions.

Tired of having their town torn up by rabble-rousers, Las Animas enacted a rule that everyone must check their weapons at the marshal's office. Never conformists, Clay and John ignored this rule, as they noticed it was not being strictly enforced with the other men in the saloons. They continued their tour of the town's saloons, all under the watchful eye of Marshal Charles Faber, who had developed a healthy hate for Clay. The lawman stated publicly if Allison "created any disturbance which would justify getting the drop on him, he would not hesitate to shoot to kill unless Allison immediately gave himself over to the marshal with lamblike docility."

The Allison brothers were in a raucous holiday mood as they entered the Las Animas dance hall that December evening, and for once, they were not drinking to excess. The Allisons clearly loved to dance, and the saloon girls were happy to oblige. Marshal Faber was not in such a festive mood when he

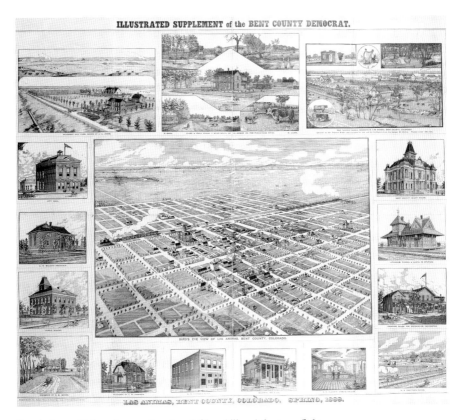

Las Animas, Colorado, was the site of Clay Allison's last gunfight.

noticed the brothers were still wearing their firearms. As Faber approached the men, he demanded they remove their weapons. Clay glanced around the dance hall and saw everyone else was allowed to wear their guns, so he posed the question to the marshal.

As was Clay's habit, the more he drank, the fewer pieces of clothing he wore. By the time Farber confronted them with his gun, both he and John were completely naked, sans their gun belts and ribbons tied around their manhoods. It is also said Clay had proceeded to humiliate the marshal by forcing him to dance and drink some alcohol, which surely did not sit well with the already upset lawman. Faber left the saloon disgraced but returned in short order with a double-barreled shotgun loaded with buckshot. As the marshal came through the door, he wordlessly took aim at John Allison. Clay saw this and called out, "Look out, John!" All three men fired their weapons simultaneously. It is said all three shots were fired in such rapid succession the reports sounded like one shot.

Marshal Faber's buckshot penetrated John's right arm and side, causing him to fall to the ground. John's and Clay's bullets were true—the marshal fell dead on the dance-hall floor with two bullets to the heart. Thinking his brother was mortally wounded, Clay grasped the hair of the fallen marshal, dragged the dead lawman over to where John was lying and said, "Look he's dead. I got him for you John." Witnesses tell of Clay crying like a baby while trying to get himself and his brother dressed.

Clay Allison refused to be arrested until John received medical attention. John was sent to Fort Lyon to be treated at the army post hospital. Seeing this, Clay made another demand: he would allow himself to be arrested only if no handcuffs or chains were used. After a promise was given, Clay allowed the arrest to take place, but the promise was immediately broken. He was chained to the wall of his jail cell.

As is the case with such incidents, potential witnesses dispersed, but it was the consensus that the marshal was looking for any excuse to harm Clay Allison and got caught in his own trap. Clay was acquitted in Charles Faber's death, as it was deemed the marshal instigated the actions and gave no warning. The Allison brothers always had each other's backs and were known gunfighters from then on. John Allison was not as good as Clay, but he was thought to have been a "better man in a fight," since he had a cool head compared to his brother's erratic behavior.

Fort Elliott Incident

After the incident in Colorado, Clay sold the Vermejo ranch to his brother John in Colfax County and left New Mexico for Texas to settle at the junction of Gageby Creek and the Washita River, near what is today Hemphill County, Texas. This move did not keep the *Cimarron News and Press* from following Clay's continued antics. On Halloween in 1878, the newspaper ran the following article. Once again, Clay Allison came to the rescue of the innocent.

> *We learn from a correspondent in Texas that R.C. Allison has been the hero of a brilliant encounter with Indians. The scene of the fight was somewhere near Fort Elliott. Allison and several ranchmen were with a company of soldiers, as volunteers. When they came in sight of the Indians, they found that the red devils had surrounded the house of an American settler and were about to massacre the family. The officer commanding the troops, thinking there was an ambush laid for his party, refused to attack.*

Left: Attacks by Natives were a constant threat at Fort Elliott, Texas.

Below: Apache, Comanche and Ute tribes fought hard to retain their lands, to no avail.

Allison, with his usual courage and daring, asked permission to lead 25 soldiers to the rescue. This was refused, and he then called for volunteers from the ranchmen. Fourteen responded to his call and, with Allison at the head, charged the Indians. They succeeded after a hot engagement, in which they had one man killed, in rescuing the family.

Allison, though his horse was shot, escaped any injury. It was a heroic affair and reflects great credit upon the gallant man who led the charge.

CANADIAN, TEXAS

Clay Allison enjoyed his time in Canadian, Texas, even though the local newspaper described the gunslinger as "hairy as a ram"—his physique was on display several times as he rode the streets in the nude. The marshal of Canadian bragged whenever Clay was in his cups what he would do when the "drunken skunk" returned. But when Allison did return, this time sober and fully clothed, the marshal demanded he relinquish his weapons.

Not one to give up his weapons, Clay promptly told the foolish lawman, "I only unlimber my guns to kill." Local legend proclaimed that Allison then forced the marshal and the "good" citizens of the town to drink so much whiskey—at gunpoint—that they became a menace to everyone else in town.

7

COMPLICATED MAN

His appearance is striking. Tall, straight as an arrow, dark-complexioned, carries himself with ease and grace, gentlemanly and courteous in manner, never betraying by work or action the history of his eventful life.
—Kinsley Graphic, *December 14, 1878*

Corpse maker.
—Stephen Zimmer

Dr. Jekyll and Mr. Hyde

Clay Allison is described as having a Jekyll-and-Hyde personality in nearly every book or article written about him. On one hand, the man was polite, honest and generous. He was often asked by local lawmen to help round up outlaws and rustlers. On the other hand, he was overbearing, unpredictable, ill-tempered and an alcoholic who could turn on a dime when he was drinking whiskey. When Clay drank heavily, it was said "the devil's lights would dance in his eyes," and his voice would drop to a barely discernable whisper. This is when Clay was thought to be at his most dangerous and deadly. In legends passed down about Clay Allison originating from both his friends and enemies, he was a complicated man.

Devil in a Duster

The nursery rhyme by Henry Wadsworth Longfellow, "There Was a Little Girl Who Had a Little Curl," states, "When she was good, she was very, very good, but when she was bad, she was horrid." This could describe our Mr. Allison. The reputations of Clay and his brother John were notorious throughout New Mexico, Texas, Colorado and Kansas. So frequent were the upheavals in saloons caused by the Allison brothers, owners took to locking their doors when news spread that the two were on a binge. The cost of the damage to lanterns, mirrors, doors and ceilings, not to mention deaths, became more than saloon owners were willing to tolerate.

Frank Cattlin, who could be termed a very lucky man, accidently knocked into Clay Allison's elbow while the latter was drinking at a bar. Upset that his whiskey was now on his shirt and the bar, Clay turned to see the man was unarmed, so he couldn't shoot him. But Clay could make an example out of the clumsy passerby. Leveling his pistol on Frank, Clay demanded he dance a jig as punishment for spilling good whiskey. Cattlin reluctantly complied as Allison shot at his feet, much to Cattlin's humiliation and the amusement of the shootist as well as nervous saloon patrons.

Clay lost interest in Cattlin and returned to drinking, not noticing his victim had left the saloon. When the cowboy returned, he approached Allison, jabbed a Colt .45 in the antagonist's ribs and demanded, "Now, damn you, you dance!" Shocked, Clay complied. Cattlin had gotten the drop on him. Clay's bad leg gave out on him after Cattlin's fourth shot, landing Allison on the floor at the cowboy's feet with his head resting on a spittoon. The humor of the situation hit Allison, who said: "Dammit boy, you've taught me a good lesson! Help me up and I'll buy you a drink!"

On cattle drives, it was customary for Clay to store five-gallon jugs of whiskey on the chuck wagon. Every evening, the men would wash away the trail dust, eat their meal and want for a better way to while away their time—they would "hug the jug and cut a rug." Since there were no women for miles, the men would dance with one another. Clay would do a war dance around the fire and let out a few rebel yells.

Las Animas, New Mexico

Being a well-liked and successful cattleman had its advantages for Clay in Las Animas, New Mexico, where he was appointed the foreman of the

As Clay Allison's drink of choice, whiskey was kept in good supply in saloons around the region. *Courtesy author's collection.*

grand jury. Much to the dismay of the court, Clay led the jury in a day-and-night session lasting twenty-eight days, during which no court business was conducted, and the jury remained consistently drunk on the whiskey the foreman had purchased.

Since this was an extended session of drinking, Clay took a short hiatus, but he returned to find court in session—without him. Surprised court attendees were stunned as he rode his "war horse" into the courtroom demanding court be adjourned until he left town again. The judge refused and ordered Allison removed. Clay answered by putting a bullet through the wall just above the judge's head. Court was immediately adjourned.

BUCKSKIN CHARLIE

Donned in his traditional buckskin suit, Buckskin Charlie became drinking buddies with Clay Allison in El Moro, New Mexico, another of the gunfighter's haunts. While trying to get Raven to drink, Clay decided Charlie was more fun. The two hit it off initially, happily drinking and carousing, but in a short time, both men became very drunk and quarrelsome.

It was agreed that no guns or knives would be used to settle the mounting argument (the reason behind the fight is not known). Clay showed Charlie no mercy, pummeling the man nearly to death. Saloon patrons pulled the men apart, seeing that Charlie was no match for Clay. A badly beaten Buckskin Charlie was taken to a nearby hospital in Trinidad, Colorado, for treatment.

CIMARRON, NEW MEXICO

Cimarron means "wild and unruly," and even with its reputation as a lawless town, it could be said that the town was not ready for Clay Allison and his cronies. Saturday nights were seen as a time to let loose, forget the burdens of the week and have fun. The cowboys took this to heart as they raced their ponies down the normally quiet streets, yelling and shooting. Citizens of this quickly growing community were getting weary of the constant regaling. Many of the town's original buildings still bear scars from the revelry.

It didn't take much to get in Clay Allison's bad favors when he was drinking, as a man known only as Wilson found out quickly. While drinking in one of Cimarron's sixteen saloons, Clay took offense at the man for

Cimarron means "wild and unruly," and this Old West town certainly lived up to its name. *Courtesy author's collection.*

some unknown reason and spent the greater part of the day in a rage looking for the elusive man.

During his search for Wilson, Allison found a law clerk by the name of John Lee, who was working at Melvin Mills's attorney's office. To extract information from the terrified clerk, Clay threw a Bowie knife straight at the man, pinning his sleeve to the door frame. Lee was able to flee the office, leaving Melvin Mills in the line of fire. Realizing this, Mills ran into Dr. Longwill's office in a panic, stating he did not know why Allison was acting so irrationally, but he feared he would have to shoot the crazed man in self-defense if Allison did not leave the office.

Dr. Longwill is said to have counseled moderation to the terrified Mills, who immediately left the doctor's office and got out of sight when he saw Allison riding toward the building. Longwill did not like Clay, having had several unpleasant encounters with him in the past, and knew what havoc he could create. Longwill stood up to Allison by telling him he was behaving badly, to which Clay replied with a laugh and said he "would do anything the doctor said to do, except he wanted Wilson's ear." The drunken man continued his search, to no avail. It is said the phantom Wilson left town soon afterward.

In Cimarron, the former Lambert's Inn, which is now the beautifully restored St. James Hotel, was victim to many of Clay Allison's antics. Many

Of the four hundred bullet holes found in the ceiling at the St. James, at least half can be attributed to Clay Allison. *Courtesy author's collection.*

stories have been told of the cattleman dancing naked on the bar and shooting up the ceiling. In Governor Miguel Otero's memoirs, he writes of attending a private poker game on the second floor of the inn, directly above the saloon, when he and his companions had to take cover around an iron stove to protect themselves from bullets penetrating the floor. In 1901, a double layer of hardwood was added to prevent anyone sleeping upstairs from being struck by gunfire.

When the St. James Hotel, owned by the Express UU Bar Ranch, was restored in 2009, more than four hundred bullet holes were discovered under the more recent tin ceiling tiles. You can bet that most of them were placed there by Clay Allison. More than twenty holes are still visible in the ceiling tiles today.

VIGILANTE, AGAIN

Clay Allison was said to have been one of the major players in a truly twisted event in the history of the New Mexico Territory. In the fall of 1870, Clay and Davy Crockett were drinking in one of the seven saloons in the gold-mining town of Elizabethtown (or E Town) when a half-frozen woman broke through the door. Hysterical and in tears, the woman relayed a story of horror to Clay, Davy and the other people in the bar.

She was Dulcinea Maldonado, the wife of a trading post owner, Charles Kennedy (or Cannady), who had a cabin in the Palo Fletchado Pass, approximately twelve miles from Elizabethtown. There, Kennedy would take in travelers and provide them with a place to stay and a meal. Kennedy's wife told how she was afraid of him and how he had threatened her if she left, but recent events were the final breaking point for the woman.

A gentleman had stopped for the night and, during casual conversation, asked if they had any trouble with Indians in the area. To which the Kennedys' seven-year-old son popped off, stating, "Yeah, can't you smell the one Papa put under the floor?" Enraged by his son's statement, Charles Kennedy shot the traveler and rammed his son's head into the rock fireplace, killing them both. He then placed their bodies in the cellar. Horrified, Dulcinea became panic-stricken, so Charles locked her in the house while he proceeded to fall into a drunken stupor. Managing to escape, reportedly up the chimney, Dulcinea traveled the long distance in the frigid cold to get help.

After hearing the woman's story, Clay, Davy and a group of men who had been stranded in John Pearson's cantina to ride out the snowstorm, rode to Kennedy's place with law enforcement. After the charred bones and bodies of the traveler, the son, as well as at least fourteen others were located, Kennedy was taken into custody. It is thought when all was said and done, Kennedy was responsible for over one hundred deaths, including possibly three more of his own children.

The young, zealous attorney named Melvin W. Mills was assigned to Charles Kennedy's case. Mills was determined to get the man acquitted. A pretrial proceeding was held on October 3, 1870. A witness stepped forward to say he had seen Kennedy shoot one of his victims. Although the court ordered action be taken by a grand jury, rumors began to circulate Mills was going to buy Kennedy's freedom. Hearing this, Clay formed a vigilante group, broke the serial killer out of jail and proceeded to hang him. (According to one of Clay's descendants, Gerry Clay Allison, this took place in an old slaughterhouse.) The group then dragged the body behind Clay's

horse on the main street of Elizabethtown. The final touch was added by Clay, who decapitated the body, placing Kennedy's head in a sack, which he draped over his saddle horn. Clay then transported it to Cimarron, twenty-nine miles away. It is said Allison demanded the head be placed on a fence stack in front of Lambert's Inn (now the St. James Hotel).

Local lore states that after a time, the gruesome head was taken to the farthest corner of the corral fence and, when it dried out completely, was then sent to the Smithsonian Institution in Washington, D.C. At the time, scientists were studying if skull formations could indicate criminal propensities in people.

The facts of this incident have been debated in recent years, since Lambert's Inn was not built by Henri Lambert until 1872. It is now thought that the head may have been staked outside the saloon in Elizabethtown. Kennedy's body was not allowed to be buried in the Catholic cemetery but was interred far outside the gate.

Opposite: The tiny mining town of Elizabethtown was home to one of the territory's first serial killers.

Above: Citizens of Elizabethtown did not allow Charles Kennedy to be buried within the gates of their cemetery. *Courtesy author's collection.*

PRANKSTER

Although Clay Allison insisted he never stole livestock, an incident on April 30, 1871, would put those statements into question. Clay, along with two companions, one being Davy Crockett (the great-nephew of the famous Alamo's "King of the Wild Frontier"), decided to remove twelve mules from the possession of Fort Union, New Mexico, which was under the Union command of General Gordon Granger. This operation went so well the stunt was attempted again in the fall. This time, however, the soldiers were alerted and ran to the corral to intervene. Confusion ensued. It was during this time the great gunfighter accidently shot himself in the right foot, creating a lifetime of pain for himself. This was the only time in Clay Allison's life that he received a gunshot wound.

The thieves were able to make it to their hideout near the Red River, where Allison sent Crockett to get Dr. Robert Longwill from Cimarron to help him with the bullet wound—the same Longwill who would cause him anguish in the Colfax County War a few years later. Due to the severity of the injury, the doctor informed Clay he must be treated in Cimarron, as there were better facilities there, much to the injured man's protests.

This injury resulted in Allison being left with a permanent limp. He often

The only time Clay Allison was shot was by his own hand while trying to steal mules at Fort Union.

used his rifle as a crutch for support later in life. Nearly every biography of Clay Allison states that he was born with a clubfoot, but family histories do not support this. This is more likely another legend or rumor. Injuries from the knife duel and this incident certainly contributed to his noticeable limited stride.

As the owner-foreman for many cattle drives, Clay Allison had the ability to bring anyone he wanted along on the trail. With a great love for music, a fiddler often accompanied the cowboys. Clay loved to dance. Some of the cowboys had to be forced by gunpoint to join in on the festivities, but all would participate at some point. One of Clay's cooks, who was obese, did not like to dance, so he would hide away until the men stopped for the night.

Millions of head of cattle were moved across the landscape of New Mexico, Texas, Kansas and Colorado.

When Allison found him lying in the tall prairie grass, he forced the rotund man to be a ballerina by the light of the moon and by gunpoint.

Allison was said to have been opposed to organizations established by livestock men because they intruded on private rights. He reportedly told a reporter of the *Las Vegas Optic* that he wished a portrait of his shepherd dog could appear with pictures of the Lincoln County Stock Association, since he felt that "the dog does not talk much but thinks a great deal" and would be an asset.

As a natural prankster, Clay would mix up bedrolls and boots and even loosen saddle girths. The new cowboys, who most likely were terrified of their boss, would be sent on impossible errands just for Allison's amusement. But none dared object. Although no one said this directly to his face, Clay was often said to be "nuttier than a Corsicana fruitcake."

EL MORO, COLORADO

In El Moro, Clay Allison enjoyed provoking men from the East who thought themselves "hard." It was Clay's great delight to cut these men down a notch or two. One such man was a newcomer from Kansas City, Jim Burns, who touted a reputation as a tough citizen in his hometown.

With money to burn, Clay visited saloons and put on displays of his expertise with his revolvers, such as shooting out the lights or taking out an entire line of glassware with one shot. He was always kind enough to pay for the damages along the way. At Jim Burns' saloon, noted as "fancy" by El Moro standards, Clay faced the owner and asked him to stand up straight against the mirror. Possibly out of fear, Burns complied.

Clay said, "Now don't you move, for I'm not going to hurt you, but just for luck I'll clip that curl off the left side of your head." Before Burns could react, Allison had already planted a few bullets within an eighth of an inch of the frightened bartender's head. After this display, the Kansas City native was made to bow to the spectators while holding up one hand and then the other. Shattered glassware and broken liquor bottles were the other victims of Allison's shenanigans. But true to form, a check for $400 arrived the next day to the Burns establishment.

DR. MENGER'S HAT

One thing could be said about Clay Allison: he had his likes and dislikes. And one had better hope that they were on the like list. Dr. Menger of El Moro, New Mexico, was a likeable man, but Clay took a strong dislike to his stovepipe hat. This distinctive hat most likely reminded the southern gentleman of the one President Abraham Lincoln wore. This did not sit too well with the former Confederate.

Each time Allison met the good doctor on the street, a comment would be made about the man getting a "proper hat," or the hat would be knocked off his head. Not able to stand the hat any longer, Clay decided to take matters into his own hands. One day, Dr. Menger passed by the saloon where the gunfighter was drinking. Clay stepped out with a shotgun and placed it against the top of the hat. One shot, and the offending headwear was gone.

As it was done in good fun, Clay took the shaken doctor's arm and directed him to the mercantile, where Clay forced him to put on a Stetson. Having no choice, the doctor agreed. Clay paid the tab, and all was good in El Moro again. After the purchase, Clay insisted on Dr. Menger joining him for a drink as a sign of "good will." Such shenanigans came to be known in El Moro as "that harum-scarum Clay Allison's foolishness."

Sheriff Rinehart

After one of Clay Allison's many frays, Sheriff Isaiah Rinehart of Cimarron rode in a horse and buggy to his ranch to place him under arrest. Clay approached the sheriff and was told the lawman had a warrant for his arrest and that he was to go with him to Las Vegas. Surprisingly, Clay agreed without argument, despite Rinehart being a loyalist to the Longwill-Elkins faction of the Santa Fe Ring.

Isaiah Rinehart was installed as sheriff of Colfax County when Governor Axtell removed the presiding sheriff and good friend of Clay Allison, Orson K. Chittenden. Axtell commented that Chittenden had "failed to file the bond required by law." Chittenden, who was Pete Burleson's father-in-law, left Colfax County for Lincoln County to become a lawman there.

During the ride, a skunk crossed the road in front of the men and was immediately shot by Allison. This started a series of events. Clay dismounted, picked up the dead skunk, took it to the buggy, was able to disarm the sheriff and tied the skunk around the lawman's neck. Under Clay's orders, Sheriff Rinehart drove around the town square with Clay following behind. "Look fellows, the sheriff's got me under arrest." As the crowd laughed and pointed at the disgraced sheriff, Clay Allison loped out of town.

Rinehart spent many nights trying to corral Allison, but Clay always seemed to be able to "one-up" the sheriff, as illustrated by an instance when Allison and his buddies were drinking heavily at Lambert's Inn. Rinehart tried to get them to go home to prevent bloodshed, but the cattleman had other ideas and made Rinehart drink as well. Stories say the lawman was so inebriated he could not walk, which brought much delight to Clay Allison.

Rinehart moved to Elizabethtown from Cimarron to escape Allison's antics and then to Tascosa, Texas, where he opened a general store and changed his name from Isaiah to Ira.

Exhibitionist

One of Clay Allison's most notorious claims to fame involved his love of dancing, mostly while naked. Today they call it the Lady Godiva Syndrome—the tendency of showing off one's genitalia to noncompliant people. While in his cups, Clay's clothes had a tendency of finding the floor. At times, his brother John joined in on the fun. Exhibitionism seemed to run in the family.

Bartenders in the saloons along Clay Allison's route braced themselves for glass breakage, as he regularly shot out lanterns and glassware. *Courtesy author's collection.*

Las Animas, Colorado, was witness to this type of display whenever the brothers decided to turn the crowded dance hall where they were partying into a strip club. Both men disrobed to their birthday suits and forced the crowd to dance with them. This rabble-rousing eventually led to the death of Sheriff Charles Faber.

Clay was also famous for dancing naked on the bar in the St. James Hotel in Cimarron. Records of this historic hotel mention the famous gunfighter enjoying his dance in the buff on many occasions, between gunning down upward of nineteen men in the meantime. The hallway of the St. James features a plaque commemorating the nineteen men who are supposed to have been slain by Clay, as well as the original headstone of Reverend Franklin J. Tolby of Colfax County War fame.

As one of the most haunted hotels in New Mexico, visiting the St. James is a step back in time. Actual metal keys are used for the rooms in the original hotel, and there are albums full of "ghostly" tales left by pervious guests. In the heart of one of the most historic towns in New Mexico, the hotel is a must-see or must-stay should you find yourself in the area. Clay Allison's presence can be felt everywhere in Cimarron, so, while in the bar, be sure to toast the resident spirit, T.J. Wright, and, of course, Robert Clay Allison.

On another drunken bender, this time in Mobeetie, Texas, Clay removed everything but his boots and gun belt and rode unashamed down the main street, shooting and singing at the top of his lungs, Lady Godiva style, in all his glory. Mind you, this was after his marriage to Dora McCullough in 1881. No one could ever accuse Robert Clay Allison of being shy.

Son of a Preacher

Raised in a religious household, Clay absorbed the values preached by his father while he ran the Presbyterian circuit in Tennessee. Newspaper articles often tell of a clerical Clay Allison who, in his moods of melancholy, would force an entire saloon full of unsavory characters to sing church hymns and listen to his version of the gospel. The "Hand of God" touched Clay Allison deeply but came out only at his convenience.

According to author Howard Bryan, Clay Allison walked by the Red Brick saloon in Cimarron on Christmas Eve in 1873 and was reportedly disgusted by the revelry going on inside, despite it being normal activity for the saloon. In the spirit of the season, Clay entered with guns drawn, demanded everyone calm down and asked if anyone knew what day it was. When he did not get the correct response, the entire saloon was forced into an impromptu Christmas Eve church service, complete with hymns and prayers.

The saloon girls were eager to please Allison and led the congregation in off-key renditions of church songs they could remember.

Another occasion took place on the banks of the alkaline Pecos River in Pecos, Texas, where Clay called home until his death in 1887. After drinking the usual amount of whiskey at the local watering hole on a Sunday, Clay decided the town needed a "come to Jesus" meeting.

While in his cups, Clay Allison could be one of three ways as a drunk. He could be a somber man who found it a good time to preach to his fellow drinkers, all the while expecting them to follow along as a good congregation. Or he could be the prankster, known to torment local law enforcement by destroying their hats or forcing them to drink to excess. Finally, he could be the dangerous drunk who was, in most cases, preyed on by thrill-seekers who thought he was too drunk to react, not knowing this was when Allison was most deadly.

Included in the article "The Red-Blooded Heroes of the Frontier" by Edgar Beecher Bronson, a one-time president of the West Texas Cattle Growers' Association, is a story about the unpredictable Clay Allison is a

Although he was considered a desperado, churches, such as this one in Elizabethtown, held a soft spot in Clay's heart.

tribute to his eclectic personality. As a son of a Presbyterian preacher, Allison had moments of piety. One moment occurred in the Lone Wolf saloon in Pecos around 1886. At 10:00 a.m., Clay boldly walked into the saloon, set down his two pistols by the door and announced to the barkeep, Red Dick, that he intended to hold a church service.

Stunned patrons were soon joined by passersby who were "invited" at the end of Allison's pistol into the bar for the meeting. Soon, the bar was filled with merchants, cowboys, freighters, gamblers, thugs, railroad men and shady ladies eager to please the volatile gunfighter. Clay demanded no liquor be sold, and cards were left on the tables during this religious encounter.

Allison announced, since the town was on the banks of the Pecos River, their first hymn was going to be "Shall We Gather at the River"—and everyone had to participate. Allison must have been quite a sight as he held the Holy Bible in one hand and his revolver in the other, sweeping the room with both while spewing fire and brimstone to the wary congregation. Always a gunfighter, Clay kept his eyes open and on the group as well, even as he demanded they all kneel. The fifty to sixty patrons did their best to comply, even though only a few managed to answer the demand.

> *O Lord, this here's a might bad neck of the woods, and I reckon You know it. Fellers don't think enough of their souls to build a church, and when a parson comes here they don't treat him half white. O Lord! Make these fellers see that when they get caught in the final roundup and drove over the last divide, they don't stand no sort of show to get to stay on the heavenly ranch unless they believe and build a house to pray and preach in. Right here I subscribe a hundred dollars to build a church and if every one of these fellers don't ante up according to his means. O Lord, make it Your personal business to see that he wears the Devil's brand and earmark and never gets another drop of good spring water.*

Red Dick passed the hat after Clay's sermon about Jonah and the whale, which yielded a good amount of money toward the building of a proper church in Pecos. It is not known if the generous contributions were given to gain favor from the gun-wielding preacher or if the donors were truly moved by his fiery sermon. Strangely enough, it was during this performance Clay predicted he would die with his boots on—not knowing within a year this prophecy would come true.

Another good deed performed by the shootist involved an anxious young man Allison found at a cow camp who had a crippled arm. The man told Allison he and another cowboy had an argument over a maverick they both claimed and had agreed to settle the dispute over a duel the next day. Understanding the man had no chance in getting his weapon unholstered in time, Clay offered to go in his place.

As the opponent rode up the next morning to get the drop on the crippled cowboy, he was shocked to see it was the famous Clay Allison he would be opposing. In his haste to leave, the dueler dropped his gun.

Davy Crockett

Clay would take up with Davy Crockett, who was nothing like his famous great-uncle. The two cowboys created trouble everywhere they went, leaving a trail of blood, bodies and bullet holes in their wake. As mentioned before, the two were of like minds when it came to the Union, northerners and Blacks and were not afraid to voice those opinions loud and often—many times with deadly results.

Crockett and his friend Gus Heffron became more brazen in their antics, frustrating the citizens of Cimarron, who demanded Sheriff Rinehart do something about them. The sheriff, knowing he was out of his league with the young gunfighters, enlisted postmaster John McCullough and rancher Joseph Holbrook as backup. On September 30, 1876, Crockett's luck ran out. The three avengers lay in wait for the gunmen to approach the Schwencke barn in Cimarron, located across from Lambert's Inn.

As Crockett and Heffron approached the barn on horseback, newly deputized Holbrook jumped out and demanded the pair put up their hands. Crockett laughed at the notion, telling Holbrook to "go ahead and shoot." Much to Crockett's surprise, Holbrook did. Rinehart and McCullough followed suit, causing the horses to bolt as they blasted away with their shotguns. Heffron was wounded, but not mortally, so he continued to ride away. Crockett's horse was found on the other side of the Cimarron River with his rider still in the saddle. The gunman's hands were said to be locked in such a death grip on the saddle horn that they had to be pried off.

Historian Philip Rasch offers this explanation:

> On March 24 David Crockett, Henry Goodman, and Gus Hefron [sic] had a drunken altercation with some of the troopers at Schwencke's saloon and threats were exchanged. About nine o'clock that evening three colored privates, George Small, John Hanson, and Anthony Harvey, were drinking at the St. James Hotel. As they were leaving the barroom, Crockett and his friends entered. Apparently, a collision occurred in the doorway, rough words were uttered, one of the soldiers made a move as if to seize Crockett, and all concerned went for their weapons. Fifteen or twenty shots were fired. All three of the soldiers were killed. No inquest was held. The presence of the troops appears to have been objectionable to the citizens and they pointedly rendered no aid in the Army's investigation. Late in September Crockett and Hefron [sic] returned to the village and ran the town for two days. On the night of the thirtieth Sheriff Rinehart, Deputy Sheriff Joseph Holbrook,

As a friend of Clay Allison, young Davy Crockett met his fate as many outlaws did: with a bullet. Davy's actual grave location is lost to history. *Courtesy author's collection.*

and John McCullough killed Crockett and wounded Hefron [sic]. The latter was captured and jailed but escaped on October 3 and seems to have disappeared from the area.

This is where the versions of Davy Crockett's death vary between historians and family lore. Family claims Rinehart, who was a member of the Santa Fe Ring, wanted Crockett's herd of horses. To get them, Davy was labeled a horse thief. Rinehart was afraid to confront the gunslinger alone, so he enlisted the help of the military to arrest him. When the Buffalo Soldiers attempted to do Rinehart's job, Crockett killed three of the four soldiers. This gave the sheriff an excuse to ambush him. Family lore says the sheriff waited until Crockett was leaving town and shot him in the back.

No matter which story is correct, Davy Crockett was laid out while awaiting burial. Jim and David Burleson write in their book *The Man Who Tamed Cimarron: The Wild and Unruly Life of Pete Burleson* that Clay Allison walked into the room containing the body of his friend to find several men milling around laughing while still wearing their hats. Incensed, Clay proceeded to let them know he would not allow this kind of disrespect. Pete Burleson had to physically restrain his friend from instigating a brawl in the room. The shocked men quickly removed their hats, and the room took on a somber atmosphere immediately.

Wolf of Washita

Highly intelligent, Clay Allison would not let anyone pull the wool over his eyes. He was nobody's fool. His cunning reputation spread from Kansas and Texas to New Mexico. In most cases, he was the darling of the newspapers of his era. Clay's temperament was pleasant, until he began drinking. Then, no one knew which Clay they were going to encounter.

With a reputation that often preceded him, Clay Allison was as feared as he was respected. O.S. Clark, author of *Clay Allison: Wolf of the Washita*, explains why living off the range was a dangerous existence. Fresh off the Goodnight-Loving Trail after selling cattle in Las Vegas, New Mexico, the author, Charley Shidler and Sam Hanna were camped along the trail in the Texas Panhandle. As they finished preparing a lunch of sowbelly and sourdough bread over a fire of cow chips, they noticed a dark figure riding up just beyond the cook fire, drawing their immediate attention.

Weapons of choice during Clay's days were the Winchester rifle, the Colt revolver and the Bowie knife.

As the lone rider came into view, the cowboys also noticed the man was, as they say, "loaded for bear." Armed with plenty of firepower, including Winchester rifles, two .45 Colt revolvers and several Bowie knives, the man rode up to their camp atop a "magnificent black gelding." Clark described the man as "a magnificent type of man, handsome, six feet or more tall, with a clear, keen, blue eye; well-dressed and he had the absolute qualities of a gentleman, polite in the extreme."

As the cowboys were all young and rather inexperienced in the social graces, one began to grill the stranger with "touchy questions" considered taboo in those times. The man answered slowly and deliberately. He stated he was from the Washita Country on his way to Las Vegas, New Mexico, where his brother, who was in trouble, was living. These answers struck a chord with the cowboys, as they had heard of Clay Allison from the Washita who had a "considerable reputation and name as a brave and daring character" and who, to their chagrin, was a known killer, with the deaths of twelve or thirteen men attributed to his gun.

Testing the waters, the cowboys asked this stranger if he knew or had heard of Clay Allison in that country. Avoiding the question at first, the stranger finally relented after being questioned once more. "I am Clay Allison. What are you going to do about it?" Shocked to the core by the stranger's answer, the cowboys stared at the man wide-eyed and swallowed hard. According to Clark, the men then "became the best table waiters the banks of that old Beaver Creek had ever seen." Clay was given the lion's share of the meat, extra sourdough sinkers and plenty of beans. Allison was hungry, stating that he had been living off jackrabbit for the past two or three days, so the men kept his plate filled to the brim. A dessert of prunes was offered and eagerly accepted by Clay.

After their meal, the men directed Clay as to which trail was best and helped him saddle his horse. Still starstruck and nervous, the cowboys said they were relieved to see Clay Allison "with his magnificent array of preparedness disappear over the darkening horizon." These cowboys would meet up with Allison again in New Mexico and in the Palo Pinto County area. They said each time they were pleased to have Allison as a friend.

Robert Clay Allison was on the first grand jury ever convened in Hemphill County, Texas, when he and John settled near the junction of Gageby Creek and the Washita River, close to Mobeetie. This small Texas town, originally named Sweetwater, was described by cattleman Charles Goodnight as "the hardest place I ever saw on the frontier except Cheyenne, Wyoming." According to records, Clay took charge of the proceedings, even refusing to be relieved of his weapons to enter the jury room and courthouse, despite a town ordinance in effect. No one dared to argue with Clay Allison, even the law.

Trail Boss

All his years driving cattle gave Clay Allison a certain sixth sense with the animals. He could read their mannerisms, and this allowed him to stay ahead of the herd, so to speak. As a trail boss, Clay checked all the boxes, writes F. Stanley. "A Trail Boss must risk his life in midnight stampedes, he is expected to expose himself to greater danger than his men, must be fearless in the face of danger with the native tribes, a Trail Boss' word was law, he must maintain the respect of his men even if this required to punch the fear of the Lord into some bullies who were as hard to handle as the cattle."

Allison could sing and was often called on to cheer up the men at the campfire with a bawdy song. He made it a rule to never make an enemy in the outfit in which he worked. Allison learned the cattle business quickly and saw an opportunity to go from a cattle driver to a cattle buyer in a few short years. As a man who was always described as extremely personable—unless he was drinking—Clay was able to broker some large deals, which put him in the same status as Goodnight and John Chisum, who were often called cattle barons.

DODGE CITY PEACE COMMISSION

What really happened between Wyatt Earp, Bat Masterson and Clay Allison in Dodge City, Kansas? Many versions of the tale exist, and they are similar. The only variations of the story are how the author of that version looked to the public. Law enforcement in Dodge City was becoming more difficult by the day, even for notable lawmen like Earp and Masterson.

With the formation of the Dodge City Peace Commission, ruffians were put on notice the town was not going to put up with their poor behavior.

The *Hays Sentinel* carried this item on September 20, 1876: "The citizens of Dodge have organized a vigilance committee and last week the committee addressed the following pointed note to every gambler in the city; 'Sir: You are hereby notified to leave this city before 6 o'clock, a.m. of Sept. 17th, 1876, and not return here.'"

Unfortunately, this authority and the scathing newspaper editorials touting the failure of the police to suppress "thieves, confidence men and robbers" pushed the police to overreact at times, taking their new orders to the extreme. Instead of a rabble-rouser being taken to jail, he was beaten mercilessly or shot dead. In March 1877, this was the case for George Hoy, one of Clay's men who came to town after the cattle drive to have some fun. Instead, he ended up dead without provocation. He had been shooting a pistol into the air in celebration.

In a blinding rage, Clay, it is said, rode three hundred miles to Dodge City on his cream-colored warhorse to settle the score with Bat Masterson and Wyatt Earp for the killing of his man. Charlie Siringo, a Pinkerton agent, wrote in his account of the story that as news of this vendetta ride spread before Allison's arrival, Masterson found a reason to leave town. The then-unknown Earp remained to deal with the psycho cowboy. Earp wrote a much different story later in life.

An ordinance was enacted in Dodge City that all weapons must be removed before entering the town. When Clay was approached to disarm during a supply run to the city, his response was typical of him: "Gentlemen, when these pistols go off they will go off smoking." Knowing the gunfighter's reputation, he was given a reprieve and allowed to carry his firearms in the town. This privilege was not abused by Clay, so he had already set a precedent that the authorities knew he would not allow to be recanted.

Allison, known as a dangerously unpredictable shooter, was a highly feared man when he graced the streets of Dodge City with his presence in 1878. He cut a striking figure, dressed in a white shirt, showy white buckskin vest with silver conchos and a black coat. Local newspapers sang his praises and then ran him through the wringer with equal vigor. Wanting an explanation and revenge for the death of one of his men, Allison spread the word that he was gunning for the lawman who killed his man. That man was Assistant Marshal Wyatt Earp.

In a letter dated at Lewistown, Montana, September 30, 1934, cowboy Pink Simms wrote:

> A drunken cowboy had been shot to death while shooting a pistol in the air in the streets of Dodge. He worked for, or at least, was a friend of, Clay Allison. Others had been robbed, shot, and beaten over the head with revolvers and the cowmen were indignant about it. It was stated that the marshals were all pimps, gamblers and saloonkeepers. They had the cowboys disarmed, and with their teeth pulled they were harmless. If they got too bad or went and got a gun, they were cut down with shotguns. Allison…[was] going to protest over the treatment of [his] men and of course the salty old Clay was willing to back his arguments with gunsmoke.

The first known written record of the Allison/Earp clash is an interview with Wyatt Earp published in the *San Francisco Examiner* of August 16, 1896. The pertinent part of the article is the following:

> And so Clay Allison came to town, and for a whole day behaved like a veritable chesterfield [perfect gentleman]. But the next morning one of my policemen woke me up to tell me that the bad man from Colorado was loaded up with a pair of six-shooters and a mouth full of threats. Straightway I put my guns on and went down the street with Bat Masterson. Now, Bat had a shotgun in the District Attorney's office, which was behind a drugstore just opposite Wright's store. He thought the weapon might come in handy in case of trouble, so he skipped across the street to get it. But not caring to be seen with such a weapon before there was any occasion for it, he stayed over there, talking to some people outside the drugstore, while I went into Webster's Saloon looking for Allison. I saw at a glance that my

man wasn't there and had just reached the sidewalk to turn into the Long Branch, next door, when I met him face to face. We greeted each other with caution…and as we spoke backed carelessly up against the wall, I on the right. There we stood, measuring each other with sideways glances. An onlooker across the street might have thought we were old friends.

This interview with Wyatt Earp appeared in the *Examiner* eighteen years after the fact, so his memory may not have been as sharp as Earp liked to believe. J. Frank Dobie wrote that Earp biographer Stuart N. Lake described Earp's reaction to Clay's leaving town as Clay and the other southerners having "backed down and [ran] out of town like so many scalded dogs." But this was written at least fifty years after the event.

Earp would continue saying that Clay Allison was "always unsure of himself, so his ruthless, neurotic mind was constantly scheming to get a decisive edge on a dangerous opponent." This may be why it is said that Earp faced Allison while carrying his Buntine Special Presentation Colt .45 with a twelve-inch barrel at the ready. Others say Chalk Beeson, owner of the Long Branch Saloon, and Turkey Track Ranch owner and cattleman Dick McNulty intervened and convinced the gunmen to put down their weapons. The possibility that Wyatt Earp never had an encounter with Allison is also an option.

Clay wanted to avenge the death of George Hoy and put Dodge City law enforcement on notice that this type of treatment of the cowmen who supplied most of the income for the Cowtown would not be tolerated. Both sides had hidden forces throughout Dodge with rifles ready for any action.

Norman Wiltsey, in a *True West* article, "Laughing Killer!," offers a dramatic rendition of what Wyatt Earp said of his encounter with the famous Clay Allison.

Earp stopped short at sight of Allison and leaned against the wall of the saloon, thus forcing Clay to approach him from in front. Around the two crack gun-slingers space was suddenly cleared as if an invisible giant hand had whisked away the apprehensive bystanders.

Allison advanced mincingly in his fancy high-heeled boots.

"You Earp?" he demanded.

"I'm Marshal Earp." Corrected Wyatt significantly.

Clay strutted closer. "I've been looking for you."

"You've found me, then."

Allison lurched suddenly against Earp; the marshal felt Clay's stomach muscles tighten as he went for his gun. He hadn't cleared leather when the muzzle of Earp's "Bluntline Special"—a presentation .45 Colt with a twelve-inch barrel—prodded Clay in the belly.

"Drop it Clay!" snapped Wyatt

Allison dropped the half-drawn weapon back into its holster as though it was red-hot. "Hell Wyatt, I was only jokin'," he grinned.

Earp failed to smile. "Get out of Dodge and take your jokes with you." He suggested grimly.

Clay wheeled, climbed aboard his cream-white horse, and left town on the gallop. His humiliation was complete; he never made trouble in Dodge again.

This account seems unlikely, as another version, written by Pinkerton agent Charlie Siringo, states that Allison did not come to Dodge City alone. He had twenty-five armed men with him as backup.

Siringo writes:

About the first of October eight hundred fat steers were cut out of my four herds and started for Dodge City, Kansas....I secured permission [from owner David T. Beals] *to...accompany them to Chicago....*

A 25-mile ride brought us to the toughest town on earth, Dodge City. It was now daylight, and the first man on the main street was Cape Willingham, who at this writing is a prosperous cattle broker in El Paso, Texas. Cape gave us our first news of the great Indian outbreak [Dull Knife's raid through Kansas]. *He told of the many murders committed by the reds south of Dodge City the day previous—one man was killed at Mead City, and two others near the Crooked Creek store. "Riding up the main street Ferris and I saw twenty-five mounted cowboys, holding rifles in their hands, and facing one of the half-dozen saloons, adjoining each other, on that side of the street* [Front Street]. *In passing this armed crowd one of them recognized me. Calling me by name he said: "Fall in line quick, h--l is going to pop in a few minutes."*

We jerked our Winchester rifles from the scabbards and fell in line, like most any other fool cowboys would have done. In a moment Clay Allison, the man-killer, came out of one of the saloons holding a pistol in his hand. With him was Mr. McNulty, owner of the large Panhandle "Turkey-track" cattle outfit. Clay was hunting for some of the town policemen, or the city marshal, so as to wipe them off the face of the earth. His twenty-five cowboy friends had promised to help him clean up Dodge City.

After all the saloons had been searched, Mr. McNulty succeeded in getting Clay to bed at the Bob Wright Hotel. Then we all dispersed. Soon after, the city law officers began to crawl out of their hiding places and appear on the street.

The actual truth of this encounter may never be known, but it is interesting to note that Wyatt Earp was careful to not publish his account of the alleged meeting until long after Clay Allison had met his death in 1887.

St. Louis Altercation

Newspaper accounts of an altercation Clay Allison had in St. Louis, Missouri, are sketchy, but it was significant enough that several mentions were made of Clay's health in the editions. This fight seemed to garner explanation from Allison himself, as he penned the following letter to the editor of the *Globe*.

A CARD FROM CLAY ALLISON.
To the Editor of the Globe:
About the 26th of July there appeared in one of the St. Louis papers an account of an altercation between myself and one Tisinger, in East St. Louis, in which account there appeared several gross misrepresentations which I desire to contradict.

1st It was alleged that I was murderer of fifteen men. In answer to this assertion, I will say that it is entirely false, and that I stand ready at all times and places for an open inspection, and anyone who wishes to learn of my past record can make inquiries of any of the leading citizens of Wayne county, Tennessee, where I was born and raised, or of officers of the late rebellion, on either side. I served in the 9th Tennessee regiment, Co. F, and the last two years of the service was a scout for Ben McCulloch and Gen. Forrest. Since the war I have resided in [New] Mexico, Texas, and Kansas, principally on the frontier, and I will refer to any of the taxpayers and prominent men in either of the localities where I have resided. I have at all times tried to use my influence toward protecting the property holders and substantial men of the country from thieves, outlaws, and murderers, among whom I do not care to be classed.

2nd, It was also charged that I endeavored to use a gun on the occasion of the St. Louis difficulty, which is untrue, and can be proven by either Col. Hunter, of St. Louis, or the clerk of Irwin, Allen & Co. It was also stated that I got the worst of the fight. In regard to this I also refer to Col. Hunter. I do not claim to be prize fighter, but as evidence of the correct result of this fight. I will only say that I was somewhat hurt but did not squeal, as did my three opponents.

My present residence is on the Washita in Hemphill County, Texas, where I am open for inspection and can be seen at any time.
Clay Allison.
Dodge City, Feb. 26, 1880.
St. Louis and other papers please copy.

Not a Ladies' Man

Although considered good-looking, charming when sober and a man of means, Clay Allison was not known as a ladies' man. His shy nature when he was young prevented him from being forward with women. In his twenties, his reputation was his downfall, as the mothers of eligible young ladies of town heard of this dashing cowboy's antics and did not want this type of man for their daughters.

Rumors persisted in local news articles of the time that Clay was extremely popular with the shady ladies of the towns he frequented, so much so that he contracted a special gift and would go to Trinidad, Colorado, to be treated for venereal disease, as that town had the best doctors. Of course, these articles were written well after Clay's death. It is certain that no one would have accused the gunslinger of this while he was alive.

One such example was with the beautiful Josephine Mary Bishop, sixteen years Clay's junior, of Las Vegas, New Mexico. Clay, dressed in his finest "Sunday Meeting" clothes, turned his efforts to courting Bishop in the mid-1870s. According to Chuck Tyrell in his blog *Western Fictioneers*, "When he went courting, her mother chased him out of the house with a broom. Apparently, she wanted someone for her daughter with skills beside knife and gun." Mrs. Bishop must have been pleased, as Josephine went on to marry attorney Frank Springer in October 1876. The town of Springer, New Mexico, is named in Frank's honor.

Carrie Gale Sexton, said to be originally from Elkhorn, Wisconsin, then living in Colfax County, was the next to draw the attention of the tall cowboy from Tennessee. But she, too, turned him down, in favor of Marion Littrell. He would be one of the few men to face Allison and humble him. Littrell was elected sheriff of Colfax County in 1894 but was a well-liked cattleman from 1869 to 1881 in Texas and in the employment of the Maxwell Land Grant in Vermejo, New Mexico, near the Allison ranch, beginning in 1881. Marion and Carrie would go on to have five children before her death at the age of eighty-four in 1941.

AMERICA MEDORA "DORA" MCCULLOUGH

Clay Allison would finally find his ladylove on the Vermejo ranch in 1873, but he did not marry her until February 15, 1881, in Mobeetie, Texas. America Medora "Dora" McCullough (sometimes spelled McCulloch) and her younger sister Kate were Civil War orphans born in Sedalia, Missouri. They were being raised by the A.J. Young family. When Clay and his brother John met the McCullough sisters, each became smitten. Reportedly, the Youngs liked John Allison but were not sure about Clay, as his reputation preceded him.

The disapproval did not stop the young couple from eloping, only to beg forgiveness when they returned. Eventually, the foster family began to like Clay, who was older than Dora by twenty-one years, and they noted that Clay was not the aggressor in the trouble that seemed to follow him like a dark cloud. Miss Patti Dora Allison was born on August 9, 1885, in Cimarron, New Mexico, and is said to have had a calming effect on her troubled father.

Clay and Dora Allison were married on February 15, 1881, in Mobeetie, Texas.

It is written that Patti was sickly as a child and that her parents often took her to the doctors in Las Vegas, New Mexico, for treatment. It was during one of these trips, writes Miguel Otero, that Clay asked him to be his bodyguard during his stay, as Clay had made too many enemies in the wild frontier town.

Another cruel tale appeared in later newspaper articles about little Patti. "He [Clay] paid in suffering when his firstborn child arrived cruelly deformed in the body; he paid in bitter remorse throughout the long nights when he couldn't sleep and drove his matched team of trotters to a steaming lather across the dark countryside."

This simply was not true. Patti Dora grew up in the lap of luxury in Fort Worth, attending luncheons with her mother and sister Clay Pearl, was the belle of debutant balls and was said to be a celebrated social butterfly of the town. Patti's beauty was lauded in the social pages of Fort Worth newspapers. She went on to marry Edmund P. Byars, bear three children and pass away at the age of eighty-six in Fort Worth.

Clay Pearl Allison, named for her famous father, would never know her namesake, as he died six months prior to her birth on February 10, 1888, in Pecos, Texas. Clay Pearl joined her sister Patti in the debutant social circles, attending many parties, which was the custom at that time. Clay Pearl's life was good with her marriage to James L. Parker and the birth of their three sons. But in her seventy-fourth year, she and her granddaughter were killed in an automobile accident. This set off a string of tragic incidents in her family that mirrored her famous father's turbulent life.

LINCOLN COUNTY, NEW MEXICO

In a 1899 article featured in the *Yorkville Enquirer* of York, South Carolina, originally run in the *New York Sun*, the unnamed author wrote that, after the killing of Pancho Griego in Cimarron, New Mexico, Clay Allison moved to southeastern New Mexico on the Pecos River, "where he bought or took charge of the Widow McSwayne's [*sic*; McSween's] cattle. Her husband had been killed in one of the cattle wars [Lincoln County War] that were part of New Mexico's history in those days, and it needed a man like Allison to keep the stock from becoming public property. Allison had married and be now settled down to live in peace, if he could, on his ranch."

Susan McSween Barber was known as the "Cattle Queen of New Mexico," as she owned the Three Rivers Cattle Company on which she ran upward of three thousand to eight thousand head of cattle on 1,158 acres of land in Lincoln County. Susan was married to Alexander McSween. An attorney for both John Chisum and John Tunstall, McSween was killed in the Lincoln County War when he stood up for Tunstall with New Mexico outlaw Billy the Kid against the Murphy-Dolan faction.

The McSween house was burned during the battle that followed the death of John Tunstall, rendering Susan homeless and determined to see the men responsible brought to justice. Attorney Huston Chapman was hired by Susan, but unfortunately, he was to meet a fate like Alexander, as he was shot at point-blank range on the "most dangerous street in

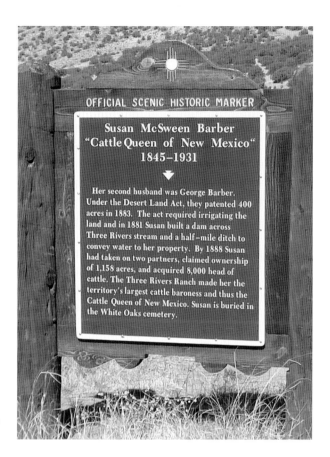

OFFICIAL SCENIC HISTORIC MARKER

Susan McSween Barber
"Cattle Queen of New Mexico"
1845–1931

Her second husband was George Barber.
Under the Desert Land Act, they patented 400
acres in 1883. The act required irrigating the
land and in 1881 Susan built a dam across
Three Rivers stream and a half–mile ditch to
convey water to her property. By 1888 Susan
had taken on two partners, claimed ownership
of 1,158 acres, and acquired 8,000 head of
cattle. The Three Rivers Ranch made her the
territory's largest cattle baroness and thus the
Cattle Queen of New Mexico. Susan is buried in
the White Oaks cemetery.

Susan McSween Barber, a survivor of the Lincoln County War, was known as a cattle queen. *Courtesy author's collection.*

America." The firearm was so close, in fact, the gunpowder ignited his clothing, and he was left to burn on the side of the street on February 18, 1879. Although several men were accused of the murder, no one was indicted in the attorney's death.

Susan McSween married and later divorced George Barber, who worked for the cattle baron John Chisum. It would be with the wedding gift of between forty and two hundred head of cattle, depending on sources, from Chisum that Susan started her own cattle empire near the gold-mining town of White Oaks, New Mexico. A New York newspaper reported Susan managed her ranch entirely on her own and built her adobe home and dam of the Three Rivers stream by hand.

A proud woman, Susan is said to have owned many pieces of diamond jewelry given to her by her husbands and admirers. She reportedly sold the jewelry over the years to survive. She died destitute in White Oaks in 1931.

Like Pulling Teeth

After a particularly grueling cattle drive from Texas to Cheyenne, Wyoming, Clay Allison's mood was worsened by an excruciating toothache. Arriving with over 1,500 head of cattle, one of Allison's first moves was to find a dentist once he got the herd and his men settled.

The Cheyenne dentist verified that the tooth giving Allison such trouble needed attention, but he worked without applying creosote to it first, as was the customary practice. During the procedure, the offending tooth was cracked in half, making it necessary for it to be extracted. Once the procedure was complete, Clay went on his way, only to find that the pain did not subside. In fact, it grew worse with the empty socket. Seeking help, the gunslinger found a new dentist, who told him the first dentist had not pulled the correct tooth.

Infuriated by the incompetence of the first dentist and at having to pay another twenty-five dollars to the second dentist, Clay returned to the first dentist on a mission. He entered the dentist's office and threw the man on the ground. Then, according to the story supposedly given to the *Las Vegas Optic* by Clay Allison personally, Clay grabbed a pair of pliers and pulled a tooth in a "tooth for a tooth" situation. The excitement of the moment overtook Clay, who went in for another tooth. This time, he attached the pliers not only to the tooth but also to the lip. The screams of the dentist brought people running, so Clay, satisfied with his work, dropped the pliers and walked away from the screaming man.

Another story handed down by a *Legends of America* source has Clay Allison realizing the wrong tooth had been extracted, pushed his way out of the chair and then went to the other dentist. After the right tooth was removed, "Clay returned to the first dentist, pushed him down into the dental chair, and pulled one of his molars with a pair of forceps. Attempting to extract a second, the dentist's screams were heard, and men came and pulled Allison away from the petrified dentist." No matter which story is correct, it is safe to say Clay Allison did not like people making mistakes at his cost.

8

STRANGE CIRCUMSTANCES
OF DEATH

Clay and Dora Allison moved to the tiny hamlet of Seven Rivers, New Mexico, which was proclaimed to be so violent that local newspapers said no one died of natural causes and you could read a newspaper at night by the light of gunfire. It was in Seven Rivers where Clay became acquainted with the Larrimore family. George Larrimore would be a player in the strange death of Clay Allison. Clay and Dora would sell their Seven Rivers ranch to purchase the Milo Pierce ranch in 1886, three years after they sold the Hemphill County ranch in Texas to John and registered the ACE brand in Texas.

This lonely rock house in the middle of nowhere near the Texas/New Mexico border had a sordid past, as it was the site of a murder. Robert "Bob" Olinger and John Jones, two players in the Lincoln County War, came to be at Louis Paxton's cow camp at the same time. Paxton was Milo Pierce's business partner in the cattle business. As Milo exited the house or chose to greet John Jones, who was the son of Barbara and Heiskell Jones, the first American settlers on the Pecos River, and a good friend of Billy the Kid, Olinger shot Jones in the back, killing him on August 29, 1879. The bullet that killed Jones traveled through his body and entered Milo Pierce's hip, crippling him for life.

Pierce would continue ranching in the desert until he decided he was spending more time fighting Indians than looking after his cattle. He was said to have knowledge of nearly every square inch of the southeastern part of New Mexico. With his health a factor and the constant threat by Native

This is one of the only remaining images of Clay's Pope's Wells ranch.

tribes, Pierce decided to move to Roswell, New Mexico, where he lived out the rest of his days.

Unlike the deaths of William H. Bonney (Billy the Kid) and Jesse James, whose demises are still hotly debated, Clay Allison was truly dead. But much like his counterparts, the circumstances of his death were widely reported by area and national newspapers, yet each had a different twist.

An article in the *Recorder* of Greenfield, Massachusetts, on July 10, 1909, tells the story of a Wild West show manager, Hollis Cooley, from Wichita, Kansas, who witnessed one of the first bullfights in the country in Dodge City, Kansas. Afterward, Cooley needed to relax and decided to go to the hot springs near Las Vegas, New Mexico. When some of the bullfight promotors found out where he was heading, they told him to give Clay Allison their best regards while there.

Unaware of the ramifications of these actions, the man went from saloon to saloon, asking the whereabouts of Clay Allison, who the article states had thirty-six notches on his gun. Cooley's questions about Allison's location were met with morbid curiosity. Saloon patrons were betting on how long this man would continue to live, being this stupid. After stating he had a message from some friends of Allison's in Dodge City, a somber, scowling man reacted to the inquiry.

"Well, I'm Clay Allison. And, say, young fellow, let me give you a piece of good advice. Never come into a bad town and ask for a bad man unless you happen to know him. I was just about to drop you when you first opened your mouth. It was the candid way you've got about you which saved your life. There is a price on my head, and I can't afford to take chances."

The article goes on to state, "Allison was killed two months later afterward, by a cowboy whose brother the desperado had shot." Several aspects of this article are false, an example of how stories develop, or blossom, over time into something unrecognizable. Clay never had a price on his head and there was never a wanted poster of any kind of him. He was not shot by a victim's brother, and it has never been proven that he killed thirty-six men.

The main facts that the different versions seem to agree on, except for the above, are a heavily loaded freight wagon lurched out of control while entering an arroyo, pitching a hapless Clay Allison off and under. This action made it possible for the wagon to roll over the neck of the shootist turned rancher, snapping it and causing a mortal wound.

One of the most widely varied accounts involve the role of alcohol in his death. Clay Allison was known as a hard drinker. Most of the violent events surrounding Allison happened while he was drinking. It was known by anyone who was familiar with the cattleman at all levels you did not antagonize a drinking Clay Allison. On the other hand, as a married man, father and soon-to-be dad, Clay was said to be trying his best to stay away from liquor. But, as with everything else in Allison's life, there were contradictions.

In one version of Clay's death, the rancher having a dispute with his neighbors over water rights. In a story by J. Frank Dobie, Clay learned that in Toyah, Texas, near his Pope's Crossing ranch, two men, Joe Nash and Jake Owen, were planning to take over Clay's watering holes just over the New Mexico Territory line. In addition to this claim, the men were said to have been talking badly about Allison—one of Clay's pet peeves and a surefire way to set the gunfighter off.

According to an oral history given by Bob Beverly to historian J. Evetts Haley of the Haley Memorial Library in Midland, Texas, in June 1938,

"He never killed a man that did not need killing" and "Gentleman Gunfighter" grace Clay Allison's headstone in Pecos, Texas. *Courtesy author's collection.*

Clay was on his way to kill Joe H. Nash and William. R. "Jake" Owen over a water dispute. Water is extremely valuable in the deserts of New Mexico and West Texas, and any infringement is seen as criminal. Nash and Owen were working a roundup for the Hashknife Ranch near Pecos, Texas.

On July 2, 1887, Clay hired a buggy and team from a livery stable to set off and speak with the gentlemen. After twenty miles in the dark, the upset rancher came upon a freighter for the Hashknife Ranch—the same ranch Nash and Owen worked for—and inquired about the men. Allison forced the freighter to get in his wagon in the dead of night to warn the men to prepare to meet their god. The freighter returned the next day, after driving all night, saying that the message had been delivered.

Clay set off for the location that day in the freighter's wagon with four mules. Allison tied his horses on the wagon and offered to drive to give the exhausted man some rest. It will never be known if this was agreeable to the freighter or if it was a forced offer. Many accounts have Clay still soaked in whiskey and furious about what he had heard.

Beverly's account has Allison, heavily drunk, upset with Nash and Owen for spreading rumors about him. He gave orders to a freighter heading to the Hashknife Ranch: "You go on up there at the round up tonight and tell them I'll be up there tomorrow and kill them and cut out their damned lying tongues out of their heads."

Beverly went on to say the freighter was so frightened he rode all night to tell Nash and Owen what Allison had said. He explained Allison "wanted to hitch his teams behind the wagon and sleep on the wagon going. He ran off one of those salt bumps and it throwed the wagon around and it throwed him out of the wagon and killed him."

In the same oral history, Bob Beverly makes a bold statement: "Clay Allison rode with Quantrill's Raiders." Clay rode with General Nathan Forrest and was reported to have become a member of the Ku Klux Klan like his mentor, but the Quantrill claim has not been substantiated. If true, the possibility of Clay Allison and Jesse James meeting is a high probability.

In an interview, Ira Gale of Trinidad, Colorado, who worked for Clay on his Vermejo ranch, gives the following account:

> *Jesse James stayed with [Dave] Moore ten months prior to 1892. He did extra work as a deputy sheriff. One time he was in Raton [New Mexico] at the Bank Exchange Saloon. Clay Allison a badman of those times came in and asked everyone to drink with him, James refused. Allison did not*

make him drink and told his followers that he "didn't like the look in that fellow's eyes."

(Dave Moore was rumored to be associated with the Quantrill's Raiders prior to Jesse James joining the band.)

The other interviewee, W. Weir, stated Billy the Kid was also introduced to twelve members of Quantrill's Raiders, of which he remarked the riders had some of the longest shotguns he had ever encountered. This has not been proven, but it is rumored James and Bonney met in Las Vegas, New Mexico, and possibly Clay Allison met them as well.

Yet another version of these events has Clay in a rage against his brother-in-law and ranch foreman, John McCullough, who was rumored to be plotting to take over Clay Allison's ranching operations. Allison heard of this plan while in Seven Rivers, New Mexico, and loudly vowed to take his revenge by killing his wife's brother. Seven Rivers rancher George Larrimore tried to talk some sense into the drunken man by explaining that this would not sit well with his wife, especially at this delicate time.

One fact most historians can agree on is that Clay was at the helm of the wagon. He was an expert drover when he was not in his cups. Whether the subsequent events played out due to his drinking is also hotly debated.

While the freighter slept, Allison sent the team into a dry arroyo but hit a clump of salt grass, which caused the wagon to jerk and the team to lurch. This action sent Clay Allison completely off the wagon and onto the arroyo bottom, almost under the wagon. The mules were spooked, lunged forward and pulled the rear wheel over Allison's neck or head, crushing it. Dobie states that Clay died instantly; others say that he lasted for nearly four hours. All agree that Clay Allison breathed his last on July 3, 1887, in the desert of West Texas.

This portrait of Clay Allison was taken just before his death in 1887 at age forty-six.

In a December 19, 1933 article in the *Albuquerque Tribune*, George Fitzpatrick states "just as Allison was breathing his last, he had some time for a few words. He said to one of the ranch hands: 'Pull off my boots quick.' As the boots were coming off, he added, 'I made up my mind to die with my boots off.' This statement is yet another twist in the life which was Clay Allison which cannot be verified." Fitzpatrick went on to say, "His dying words were probably the last gesture of a man tired of violence—whose life had been filled with violence and violent deaths."

After learning of the shootist's death, the newspapers that had such a field day with Allison's antics wrote touching tributes to the man.

> *Clay Allison, a brave, true-hearted and oft-times dangerously reckless man, when in his cups, has at last died with his boots on, but not by the pistol route. He fell from his wagon in Texas, some days ago, the wheels of the same running over his neck and breaking it. The career of Clay Allison is perhaps unparalleled in the western country and should be written up by someone Conversant with it.*
> —Las Vegas Optic, *July 26, 1887*

> *All of our old timers knew Clay Allison. He knew no fear, was a good-looking man. To incur his enmity was about equivalent to a death sentence. He contended always that he had never killed a man willingly; but that the necessity in every instance had been thrust upon him. He was expert with his revolver, and never failed to come out first best in a deadly encounter. Whether this brave, genteel border man was in truth a villain, or a gentleman is a question that many who knew him never settled to their satisfaction. Certain it is that many of these stern deeds were for the right as he understood the right to be.*
> —Dodge City Globe, *July 26, 1887*

Former Pinkerton detective and cowman Charlie Siringo also wrote a debated version of the gunfighter's death, which saw Clay Allison living in the Seven Rivers area while frequenting the store and saloon. On one occasion, Clay became quite inebriated as well as irritated in the Seven Rivers saloon, as he heard rumors being spread by a couple of neighboring ranchers. Working himself into a rage, Clay drank even more and had to be taken out of the saloon by his friend George Larrimore.

Allison slept on the back of a wagon on the way back to his ranch but woke up itching to prove to Larrimore what a fine muleskinner he was. Siringo said the mules bolted once Allison took over the reins, throwing Clay underneath the heavy wagon. His neck was broken by the wheel.

Clay's death was recounted in the July 3, 1887 edition of the *Eddy Argus*, which offered another slant on the story:

Past gunslinger Clay Allison is accidently killed near Pecos, Texas. He was run over by his own wagon. Local history says young Jack Owen of Lookout, who was working for Allison at his ranch had upset Allison, who felt that Jake was sniffing around his wife too much. Allison sent Owen a letter saying he was on his way to Lookout to kill Owen. Instead, the accident occurred. We are told that on the same evening this word reached Lookout, the Baptists held a joyful prayer meeting thanking the Lord for saving Jake and for also sending Mr. Allison on his way to Hell.

OLD RUIDOSO, GHOST STEER

One of the more far-fetched theories of Clay Allison's demise involves the legend of "Old Ruidoso" (Ruidoso translates to "noisy water"), cattleman John Chisum's ghost steer. As the story is related, the maverick steer brought death and destruction to all who were unlucky enough to meet up with this fire-snorting beast. Old Ruidoso was said to have an aggressive roar and roamed along the Pecos River, stirring up trouble. John Chisum had a habit of buying huge longhorn steers and branding them with his long rail brand before releasing them into the open range of his Jingle Bob Ranch.

Robert "Bob" Olinger, of Lincoln County War fame, reportedly came across Old Ruidoso on the range and decided to catch and brand him with the skull and crossbones and put a curse on the steer before turning him loose again. This brand gave the longhorn the reputation as a devil steer. Ironically, Olinger would be killed with his own shotgun by Billy the Kid in the Lincoln County War shortly afterward. Some say he was the first victim of his own curse.

Since Clay Allison lived in the Seven Rivers area, he most likely heard of this outlaw steer. Old-timers are convinced it was the curse that spooked Allison's mules, and the devil steer's scream caused the wagon to lurch forward, throwing Allison to the ground, where he broke his neck. The cattleman is said to have died with the knowledge his death was caused by this cursed steer.

Mescalero Apache lore supports the stories of the ranchers, who swore to have seen and heard "bloodcurdling bellows of a mad steer." Tales of death and destruction have been told in Roswell, Lincoln and Mesilla, New Mexico, as well as in Amarillo and Tascosa, Texas, all attributed to the ghost steer. Old Ruidoso may still be roaming the rangelands of southeastern New Mexico and West Texas, so stay clear of the ghost steer on dark nights if you don't want to meet the same fate as many before.

PLACE OF HONOR

After Clay's death, his body was buried in the Old Pecos Cemetery with the pioneers of the region. A permanent marker replaced the wooden cross that adorned what people thought was Allison's grave according to a 1967 article in the *Odessa American*. Barney Hubbs, a businessman, president of the West of the Pecos Museum and local historian in Pecos, Texas, made sure Clay's grave had this marker. Lifetime Pecos resident Joe Kraus and his uncle were said to have taken care of the gunfighter's grave after Dora Allison married Jesse Lee Johnson and moved to Fort Worth. They would sow wildflowers on the grave each year, and it would be a beautiful site.

Questions arose as to the exact location of Clay Allison's grave after the flood of 1920 displaced every marker in the sandy-soiled cemetery. Floods continued to cause havoc for the residents of Pecos and wiped out evidence of graves with each deluge. Today, only a few grave markers remain, including Clay's. Iron fences around a couple of graves are the only indications of a cemetery.

The sandy soil of the Old Pecos Cemetery flooded so often that graves were disinterred and reburied in other Pecos, Texas cemeteries. *Courtesy author's collection.*

A permanent marker was placed at the likely location where Robert Clay Allison was buried in the Old Pecos Cemetery. It is one of only six remaining markers. *Courtesy author's collection.*

In death as in life, Robert Clay Allison made an impression. He is said to be the only gunfighter to have his own cemetery, as he has been given a place of honor in the middle of downtown Pecos. Surrounded by red brick walls and black iron gates, the lone grave is on the grounds of the West of the Pecos Museum on Oak Street and features a granite headstone that reads, "Gentleman Gunfighter." The footstone highlights a famous quote of Allison's: "Never killed a man who did not need killing."

Love him or hate him, Robert Clay Allison left an indelible mark on the history of New Mexico and West Texas and deserves his due. The gentleman gunfighter was a product of his raising and his times, and except for a few people—mostly his victims—he was well respected by his peers. Clay Allison was a paradox of behaviors, good and bad; he stood up for what he believed to be right. His obituaries said it all: there will never be another Robert Clay Allison.

BIBLIOGRAPHY

Books

Adams, Clarence S., and Joan N. Adams. *Riders of the Pecos and the Seven Rivers Outlaws*. Roswell, NM: Old Time Publications, 1990.

Adams, Ramon F. *Burs Under the Saddle: A Second Look at Books and Histories of the West*. Norman: University of Oklahoma Press, 1989.

Allison, Jerry "Clay." *The Life and Death of a Gunfighter. Book 1, Part One*. Bloomington, IN: 1st Books Library, 2002.

Ball, Larry. *Desert Lawmen: The High Sheriffs of New Mexico and Arizona*. Albuquerque: University of New Mexico Press, 1992.

Bretham, Carl W. *Great Gunfighters of the West*. San Antonio, TX: Naylor, 1962.

Bronson, Edgar Beecher. *The Red-Blooded Heroes of the Frontier*. New York: George H. Doran Company, 1910.

Bryan, Howard. *Robbers, Rogues and Ruffians: True Tales of the Wild West in New Mexico*. Santa Fe, NM: Clear Light Publishers, 1991.

Burleson, Jim, and David Burleson. *The Man Who Tamed Cimarron: The Wild and Unruly Life of Pete Burleson*. Santa Fe, NM: Burleson Heritage Publishing, 2021.

Caffey, David L. *Chasing the Santa Fe Ring: Power and Privilege in Territorial New Mexico*. Santa Fe: University of New Mexico Press. 2015.

———. *Frank Springer and New Mexico: From the Colfax County War to the Emergence of Modern Santa Fe*. College Station: Texas A&M University Press, 2006.

Cimino, Al. *Gunfighters: A Chronicle of Dangerous Men and Violent Death*. New York: Chartwell Books, 2016.

Clagett, Thomas D. *West of Penance*. Santa Fe, NM: Rio Lobo Press, 2016.

Clark, O.S. *Clay Allison of the Washita*. Houston: Frontier Press of Texas, 1920.

Cleaveland, Agnes Morley. *No Life for a Lady*. Lincoln: University of Nebraska Press, 1977.

Cleaveland, Norman. *Colfax County's Chronic Murder Mystery*. Santa Fe, NM: Rydal, 1977.

Clifford, Frank. *Deep Trails in the Old West: A Frontier Memoir*. Edited by Frederick Nolan. Norman: University of Oklahoma Press, 2011.

Dearen, Patrick. *A Cowboy of the Pecos*. Plano, TX: Woodware Publishing, 1997.

———. *Crossing Rio Pecos*. Fort Worth: Texas Christian University Press, 1996.

Dobie, J. Frank. *The Flavor of Texas*. Dallas, TX: Dealey and Lowe, 1936.

Freiberger, Harriet. *Lucien Maxwell: Villain or Visionary*. Santa Fe, NM: Sunstone Press, 1999.

Haley, J. Evetts. *Charles Goodnight, Cowman and Plainsman*. Norman: University of Oklahoma Press, 1936.

Hendricks, George D. *The Badman of the West*. San Antonio, TX: Naylor Company, 1959.

Hogan, Ray. *The Life and Death of Clay Allison*. New York: Signet Classics, 1961.

Hubbs, Barney. *Shadows along the Pecos: Robert Clay Allison, Gentleman Gunfighter, 1840–1887*. Pecos, TX: West of the Pecos Museum, 1966.

Keleher, William A. *The Fabulous Frontier*. Santa Fe, NM: Rydal Press, 1946.

LeMay, John. *Tall Tales and Half Truths of Billy the Kid*. Charleston, SC: The History Press, 2015.

———. *Tall Tales and Half Truths of Pat Garrett*. Charleston, SC: The History Press, 2016.

McDevitt, Kevin, with Ed Sitzberger. *History of the St. James Hotel*. Colorado Springs, CO: Cimarron Press, 2019.

Metz, Leon. *The Encyclopedia of Lawmen, Outlaws and Gunfighters*. New York: Checkmark Books, 2002.

Murphy, Lawrence R. *Philmont: A History of New Mexico's Cimarron Country*. Albuquerque: University of New Mexico Press, 1972.

O'Neal, Bill. *Encyclopedia of Western Gunfighters*. Norman: University of Oklahoma Press, 1979.

Parsons, Chuck. *Clay Allison, Portrait of a Shootist*. Seagraves, TX: Pioneer Book Publishers, 1983.

———. *Outlaws and Lawmen of the Old West: The Best of NOLA*. Laramie: National Association for Outlaw and Lawman History in affiliation with the University of Wyoming, 2001.

Peters, James S. *Robert Clay Allison: Requiescat in Pace*. Santa Fe, NM: Sunstone Press, 2008.

Serna, Louis. *Clay Allison and the Colfax County War*. Cimarron, NM: Self-published, 2020.

Stanley, F. *Clay Allison*. Santa Fe, NM: Sunstone Press, 2008.

———. *Desperados of New Mexico*. Santa Fe, NM: Sunstone Press, 2015.

Trachman, Paul. *The Old West: The Gunfighters. Book 8*. New York: Time-Life Books, 1976.

Treadwell, Terry C. *Outlaws of the Wild West*. Yorkshire, UK: Frontline Books, 2021.

Truett, John A. *Clay Allison: Legend of Cimarron*. Santa Fe, NM: Sunstone Press, 2000.

Yadon, Laurence, and Dan Anderson. *200 Texas Outlaws and Lawmen, 1835–1935*. Gretna, LA: Pelican Publishing, 2008.

Articles

Brelhan, Carl W. "Clay Allison—Fantastic Gunslinger." *Western Frontier* (May 1978).

———. "Clay Allison—Psychopathic Killer." *Western Frontier* Annual no. 1 (1975).

Dobie, J. Frank. "Clay Allison of the Washita." *Frontier Times* (February 1943).

Morrison, W.B. "Colbert's Ferry on Red River, Chickasaw Nation, Indian Territory, Recollections of John Malcolm, Pioneer Ferryman." *Chronicles of Oklahoma* 16 (September 1938).

O'Dell, Lary. "Colbert's Ferry." *The Encyclopedia of Oklahoma History and Culture*. https://www.okhistory.org.

Rasch, Philip J. "The People of the Territory of New Mexico VS. The Santa Fe Ring." *New Mexico Historical Review* 47, no. 2 (2021).

Sandoval, Richard C. "Clay Allison's Cimarron," *New Mexico Magazine* (March–April 1974).

Websites

Kansas History Web Sites. http://www.kansashistory.us.
Legends of America. https://www.legendsofamerica.com.
New Mexico Nomad. https://newmexiconomad.com.
Pecos, Texas. https://visitpecos.com.
Southeastern New Mexico Historical Society. https://www. nearlovingsbend. org.

INDEX

ABOUT THE AUTHOR

Courtesy author's collection.

Exploring her home state of New Mexico is author Donna Blake Birchell's favorite pastime. Sharing the vast history of New Mexico gives her great joy, and she hopes you will find as much enjoyment in your own historical discoveries in the Land of Enchantment.